Genetic Algorithms

Genetic Algorithms

Genetic Algorithms

Bill P. Buckles and Frederick E. Petry

IEEE Computer Society Press
Los Alamitos, California

Washington • Brussels • Tokyo

IEEE Computer Society Press Technology Series

Library of Congress Cataloging-in-Publication Data

Buckles, Bill P., 1942-
    Genetic Algorithms/ Bill P. Buckles and Frederick E. Petry.
        p.   cm.
    Includes bibliographical references.
    ISBN 0-8186-2935-5 (pbk.)
        1. Genetic algorithms.   I. Petry, Fred.   II. Title.
QA402.5.B83 1992
006.3'01'5118--dc20   CIP 92-16233

Published by the
IEEE Computer Society Press
10662 Los Vaqueros Circle
PO Box 3014
Los Alamitos, CA 90720-1264

IEEE Computer Society Press Order Number 2935
Library of Congress Number 92-16233
IEEE Catalog Number EH0353-3
ISBN-8186-2935-5 (paper)
ISBN 0-8186-2936-3 (microfiche)

Additional copies can be ordered from

IEEE Computer Society Press	IEEE Service Center	IEEE Computer Society	IEEE Computer Society
Customer Service Center	445 Hoes Lane	13, avenue de l'Aquilon	Ooshima Building
10662 Los Vaqueros Circle	PO Box 1331	B-1200 Brussels	2-19-1 Minami-Aoyama
PO Box 3014	Piscataway, NJ 08855-1331	BELGIUM	Minato-ku, Tokyo 107
Los Alamitos, CA 90720-1264			JAPAN

Technical editor: Rao Vemuri
Production editor: Anne Copeland
Copy edited by Henry Ayling
Cover art by Joe Daigle
Printed in the United States of America by KNI, Inc.

The Institute of Electrical and Electronics Engineers, Inc.

Table of Contents

An Overview of Genetic Algorithms and Their Applications

Genetic algorithms (GAs) originated from the studies of cellular automata, conducted by John Holland and his colleagues at the University of Michigan. Holland's book, published in 1975 and discussed briefly in this volume's annotated bibliography, is generally acknowledged as the beginning of GA research. The consistent growth in interest since then has increased markedly during the last six years. Applications include such diverse areas as job shop scheduling, training neural nets, image feature extraction, and image feature recognition.

A GA is a search procedure modeled on the mechanics of natural selection rather than a simulated reasoning process. Domain knowledge is embedded in the abstract representation of a candidate solution termed an organism. Organisms are grouped into sets called populations. Successive populations are called generations. A generational GA creates an initial generation, $G(0)$, and for each generation, $G(t)$, generates a new one, $G(t + 1)$. An abstract view of the algorithm is

```
generate initial population, G(0);
evaluate G(0);
t : = 0;
repeat
        t : = t + 1
        generate G(t) using G(t -1);
        evaluate G(t);
until solution is found.
```

The operation "evaluate $G(t)$" refers to the assignment of a figure of merit to each of the population's organisms. In simple GAs, an alternative exists to replacing an entire population at once; that alternative is to replace one organism in the population whenever a new organism is created. This variant is known as a steady state GA.

In most applications, an organism consists of a single chromosome. A chromosome of length n is a vector of the form

$$< x_1, x_2, \dots, x_n >$$

where each x_i is an allele, or gene. The domain of values from which x_i is chosen is called the alphabet of the problem. Frequently, the alphabet used consists of the binary digits $\{0, 1\}$. We can view a specific chromosome as representative of many patterns. Using # as "don't care," an example pattern or schema over the binary alphabet is <# # 1 1 0 #>. The chromosomes <1 1 1 1 0 0> and <1 0 1 1 0 0> are specific instances of this and other schemata; for example, <1 # # 1 0 0>. The order of a schema is the number of non-# symbols it contains. Its length is the distance from the first to the last non-# position. Thus, the length of <# 1 # 0 # 1> is four, and its order is three.

GAs differ from traditional search techniques in several ways:

• First, GAs optimize the trade-off between exploring new points in the search space and exploiting the information discovered thus far. This was proven using an analogy with the k-armed bandit (an extension of the one-armed bandit) problem.[1]

• Second, GAs have the property of implicit parallelism. Implicit parallelism means that the GA's effect is equivalent to an extensive search of hyperplanes of the given space, without directly testing all hyperplane values. Each schema denotes a hyperplane.

• Third, GAs are randomized algorithms, in that they use operators whose results are governed by probability. The results for such operations are based on the value of a random number.

• Fourth, GAs operate on several solutions simultaneously, gathering information from current search points to direct subsequent search. Their ability to maintain multiple solutions concurrently makes GAs less susceptible to the problems of local maxima and noise.

As noted, GAs are randomized — but not random — search algorithms. Each organism represents a point (that is, an intersection of hyperplanes) in the search space. Randomization must balance two competing concerns, exploration and exploitation. A solution cannot be tested unless it appears as an organism. Therefore, a reasonable number of solutions must be explored. On the other hand, unlimited exploration would not be efficient search. The strength of highly fit organisms must be exploited and allowed to propagate in the population. Yet, giving too much precedence to such organisms results in premature termination at a local optimum.

We can compare GA recombination operators to controlled breeding among, say, thoroughbred horses. The objective is to combine highly fit organisms to produce a still more fit individual. Both the selection of "parents" and the steps within the recombination operators are randomized. Parent selection dynamics are based on an application-dependent measure of an organism known as the fitness function, f_i (f_i is a figure of merit, computed using any domain knowledge that applies). In principle, this is the only point in the algorithm at which domain knowledge is necessary. Organisms are chosen using the fitness value as a guide; organisms having higher fitness values are chosen more often. Selecting organisms based on fitness value is a major factor in the strength of GAs. The greater the fitness value of an organism, the more likely that the organism will be selected for recombination.

There are two popular approaches for implementing selection. The first, roulette selection, assigns a probability to each organism, i, computed as the proportion

$$F_i = f_i \,/\, \Sigma_j \, f_j$$

A parent is then randomly selected, based on this probability. A second method, deterministic sampling, assigns to each organism, i, a value

$$C_i = RND(F_i \times n) + 1$$

where n organisms reside in the population (RND means round to integer). The selection operator then assures that each organism participates as a parent exactly C_i times.

Parents participate in the later recombination operations. Alleles from the parents are mixed via an operator called a crossover rule, of which many exist. Simple one-point crossover of chromosomes from two parents at a random point, j, is illustrated by

$$< x_1 \, x_2 \, ... \, x_j \, x_{j+1} \, x_{j+2} \, ... \, x_n >$$
$$+$$
$$< y_1 \, y_2 \, ... \, y_j \, y_{j+1} \, y_{j+2} \, ... \, y_n >$$
$$=$$
$$< x_1 \, x_2 \, ... \, x_j \, y_{j+1} \, y_{j+2} \, ... \, y_n >$$

where the result is a chromosome of the offspring and is placed in the next generation.

A mutation is the random change of an allele from one alphabet value to another. For a problem over the binary alphabet, the original allele is exchanged for its complement. The mutation operator offers the opportunity for new genetic material to be introduced into a population. From the theoretical perspective, it assures that — given any population — the entire search space is connected. The new genetic material does not originate from the parents and is not introduced into the child by crossover. Rather, it occurs after crossover a small percentage of the time.

Several stopping criteria exist for the algorithm. The algorithm may be halted when all organisms in a generation are identical, when $f_i = f_j$ for all i and j, or when $|f_i\text{-}f_j| < TOL$ for some small value TOL and all i and j. An alternative criterion would halt after a fixed number of evaluations and take the best solution found.

For GAs, a significant concept is that of implicit parallelism. Implicit parallelism means that search effort is allocated simultaneously in many hyperplanes (regions) of the space. This follows from Holland's schema theorem. As noted, we can view a specific organism (list of alleles) as representative of many schemata.

The fundamental theorem of GAs (the schema theorem) explains that instances of certain more fit schemata appear with exponentially greater frequency as organisms are replaced. Schemata can also be interpreted as hyperplanes in the search space.

Suppose for a generation, $G(t)$, a population of n organisms exists, of which m organisms are instances of schema S (that is, $m_t(S)$. Recall that, with roulette-wheel selection, organisms are selected for parents based on fitness, f_i. Consequently, the number of instances of schema S at the next stage is

$$m_{t+1}(S) = m_t(S) \cdot \frac{f(S)}{f}$$

where $f(S)$ is the average fitness of organisms instantiating S, and f is the average fitness of the entire population. This equation represents exponential growth.

Next, we can analyze the effects of crossover and mutation on schemata. In general, a longer schema's survival is less likely since there is a higher probability of a crossover operation cutting it. Likewise, a schema will survive under mutation if none of its positions are changed.

Therefore, after analyzing and taking into account the effects of operators such as crossover and mutation, a factor α, $\alpha < 1$ can be obtained, leading to the relation

$$m_{t+1}(S) > m_t(S) \cdot \frac{f(S)}{f} \cdot \alpha$$

This relation implies that more fit schemata with short defining length and low order are allocated exponentially, thereby increasing representation in future generations.

Selected papers

This technology series volume contains selected papers representing GA principles and applications. The first three papers represent various issues, including implicit parallelism and the sizing of populations. The second three papers deal with aspects of GAs and learning, including the topic of classifier systems. The final three papers cover the application of GAs to pattern recognition, permutation problems, and neural nets.

A general framework for an overall classification of GAs can be based on parameters and strategies. Grefenstette's first paper describes a series of experiments that seek optimal GA strategies for a given set of numerical optimization problems. The solutions were optimized over six parameters. An interesting aspect of this approach is that the searches were done by GAs, representing metalevel optimization techniques. Next, Grefenstette and Baker examine theoretical results of applications to actual optimization problems. The authors discuss limitations of the results as well as the need for more sophisticated approaches to quantify the parallelism of GAs.

GAs balance the need to explore a reasonable proportion of the search space against the need to exploit information in high-fitness organisms. Goldberg addresses this issue in our third paper. Overemphasizing exploration leads to more organism evaluations than necessary. Overemphasizing exploitation leads to early concentration on a few individual organisms that, in combination, produce convergence to a local optimum. Large populations favor exploration, and small ones favor exploitation; it is at this level that the issue is resolved. Goldberg first derives an analytic model of convergence rate, and then searches a reasonable range of population sizes to determine the optimum schema-processing rate. The solution varies with respect to organism length.

The next three papers deal with aspects of learning using GAs. De Jong summarizes various approaches in his overview paper. He first analyzes the simplest — parameter-based techniques — then follows with variations for internal data structures; for example, those permutations required by the traveling-salesman problem. Additionally, De Jong considers dynamic behaviors, including the learning of algorithms. Conventional representations (programming languages, among others) are difficult to effectively manipulate with GAs, so production systems are commonly studied.

Two major approaches exist: In the first, each organism in the population is an entire production system algorithm; in the second, called classifier systems, individual rules are the units manipulated by GAs. De Jong describes differences in genetic operations, fitness evaluation, and credit assignment for each representation.

Holland describes the learning approach based on classifier systems. These are parallel rule-based systems that act by message passing. Learning is accomplished by either of two approaches. First, credit assignment by the bucket brigade technique (among others) can provide a way to learn from the performance of a rule set, adapting rules appropriately. Second, the discovery of new rules in the system occurs through the use of GAs. Of course, the new rules formulated can be evaluated via credit assignment techniques.

We find parameter adjustment in neural-network applications, and threshold tuning in systems with decision rules. Other forms of learning exist, of course. Spears and De Jong take a GA approach to symbolic learning; specifically, they present a system for concept learning from positive and negative examples.

We have chosen three papers to represent various application techniques and domains. Some tasks, including the routing problem, require each organism to contain exactly one copy of each allele value; that is, each organism is a permutation of the alleles, which implies that mechanisms for crossover and mutation must maintain the permutation constraint. In the first application paper, Buckles et al. describe several permutation-preserving operators. The traveling-salesman application has been studied extensively, using GAs, and domain-specific crossover operators have been developed for it. However, this paper uses only canonical permutation operators to examine the exploitation/exploration issue. The crossover operator is modified so as to preserve a fixed number of schemata. It is determined experimentally that efficiency drops whenever (1) too few schemata are saved (too much exploration), or (2) too many are saved (too much exploitation).

Canonically, a GA uses domain knowledge only within the fitness function. Selection, crossover, and mutation are independent of the application. Ankenbrandt et al. use a canonical generational GA to label features from a segmented satellite image of the North Atlantic. They represent an organism as a list of labels, one per segment, and represent features (such as nearness to or direction from other features) in the form of a semantic net. Relationships between labels in an organism are compared to nominal relationships within the net, and a fitness value is assigned based on how well the organism matches nominal relationships. The application illustrates both nonbinary alleles and the use of nonbinary alphabets.

Many techniques have been applied to the establishment of optimal weights for neural networks, including approaches based on GAs. With respect to GAs in general, either hyperplane sampling or hill climbing may be emphasized. Which approach is given preference depends upon the balance between mutation and other recombination operators. Whitley et al. discuss empirical results for control problems (inverted pendulum), indicating that genetic hill climbers are effective at neural-network weight optimization. The authors compare their approach to reinforcement learning (which uses an adaptive heuristic critic) and assess the relative merits of each.

Optimization of Control Parameters for Genetic Algorithms

JOHN J. GREFENSTETTE, MEMBER, IEEE

Abstract—The task of optimizing a complex system presents at least two levels of problems for the system designer. First, a class of optimization algorithms must be chosen that is suitable for application to the system. Second, various parameters of the optimization algorithm need to be tuned for efficiency. A class of adaptive search procedures called genetic algorithms (GA) has been used to optimize a wide variety of complex systems. GA's are applied to the second level task of identifying efficient GA's for a set of numerical optimization problems. The results are validated on an image registration problem. GA's are shown to be effective for both levels of the systems optimization problem.

I. INTRODUCTION

THE PROBLEM of dynamically controlling a complex process often reduces to a numerical function optimization problem. Each task environment for the process defines a performance response surface which must be explored in general by direct search techniques in order to locate high performance control inputs (see Fig. 1).

If the response surface is fairly simple, conventional nonlinear optimization or control theory techniques may be suitable. However, for many processes of interest, e.g. computer operating systems or system simulation programs, the response surface is difficult to search, e.g., a high-dimensional, multimodal, discontinuous, or noisy function of the control inputs. In such cases, the choice of optimization technique may not be obvious. Even when an appropriate class of optimization algorithms is available, there are usually various parameters that must be tuned, e.g., the step size in a variable metric technique. Often the choice of parameters can have significant impact on the effectiveness of the optimization algorithm [8]. The problem of tuning the primary algorithm represents a secondary, or metalevel, optimization problem (see Fig. 2).

This work attempts to determine the optimal control parameters for a class of global optimization procedures called genetic algorithms (GA's). The class of GA's is distinguished from other optimization techniques by the use of concepts from population genetics to guide the search. However, like other classes of algorithms, GA's differ from one another with respect to several parameters and strategies. This paper describes experiments that search

Manuscript received March 21, 1984; revised August 28, 1985. This work was supported in part by a Fellowship from the Vanderbilt University Research Council and by the national Science Foundation under Grant MCS-8305693.

The author is with the Computer Science Department, Vanderbilt University, Nashville, TN 37235, USA.

IEEE Log Number 8406073.

Reprinted from *IEEE Transactions on Systems, Man, and Cybernetics*, 16, Number 1, 1986, pages 122-128. Copyright ©

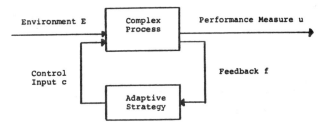

Fig. 1   One-level adaptive system model.

a parameterized space of GA's in order to identify efficient GA's for the task of optimizing a set of numerical functions. This search is performed by a metalevel GA. Thus GA's are shown to be suitable for both levels of the system optimization problem.

The remainder of this paper is organized as follows: Section II contains a brief overview of GA's and a summary of previous work. Section III describes the design of experiments which test the performance of GA's as metalevel optimization strategies. The experimental results appear in Section IV. A validation study is presented in Section V. The conclusions are summarized in Section VI.

II. OVERVIEW OF GENETIC ALGORITHMS

Suppose we desire to optimize a process having a response surface u, which depends on some input vector x. It is assumed that no initial information is available concerning the surface u, but that a black box evaluation procedure can be invoked to compute the scalar function $u(x)$. The state of the art in such situations is to perform some sort of random search, perhaps combined with local hill-climbing procedures [5], [9]. Genetic algorithms are global optimization techniques that avoid many of the shortcomings exhibited by local search techniques on difficult search spaces.

A GA is an iterative procedure which maintains a constant-size population $P(t)$ of candidate solutions. During each iteration step, called a *generation*, the structures in the current population are evaluated, and, on the basis of those evaluations, a new population of candidate solutions is formed (see Fig. 3.)

The initial population $P(0)$ can be chosen heuristically or at random. The structures of the population $P(t + 1)$ are chosen from $P(t)$ by a randomized selection procedure that ensures that the expected number of times a structure is chosen is approximately proportional to that structure's

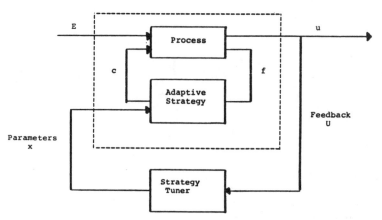

Fig. 2   Two-level adaptive system model.

```
t <- 0;
initialize P(t); -- P(t) is the population at time t
evaluate P(t);
while (termination condition not satisfied) do
begin
        t <- t+1;
        select P(t);
        recombine P(t);
        evaluate P(t);
end;
```

Fig. 3   Skeleton of a genetic algorithm.

performance relative to the rest of the population. In order to search other points in the search space, some variation is introduced into the new population by means of idealized *genetic recombination operators*. The most important recombinational operator is called *crossover*. Under the crossover operator, two structures in the new population exchange portions of their internal representation. For example, if the structures are represented as binary strings, crossover can be implemented by choosing a point at random, called the crossover point, and exchanging the segments to the right of this point. Let $x_1 = 100{:}01010$ and $x_2 = 010{:}10100$, and suppose that the crossover point has been chosen as indicated. The resulting structures would be $y_1 = 100{:}10100$ and y_2 $010{:}01010$.

Crossover serves two complementary search functions. First, it provides new points for further testing within the hyperplanes already represented in the population. In the above example, both x_1 and y_1 are representatives of the hyperplane 100#####, where the # is a "don't care" symbol. Thus, by evaluating y_1, the GA gathers further knowledge about this hyperplane. Second, crossover introduces representatives of new hyperplanes into the population. In the previous example, y_2 is a representative of the hyperplane #1001###, which is not represented by either parent structure. If this hyperplane is a high-performance area of the search space, the evaluation of y_2 will lead to further exploration in this subspace. Each evaluation of a structure of length L contributes knowledge about the performance of the 2^L hyperplanes represented by that structure. The power of GA's derives largely from their ability to exploit efficiently this vast amount of accumulating knowledge by means of relatively simple selection mechanisms [17]. Termination of the GA may be triggered by finding an acceptable approximate solution, by fixing the total number of structure evalu-

ations, or some other application dependent criterion. For a more thorough introduction to GA's [7], [17].

As stated above, GA's are essentially unconstrained search procedures within the given representation space. Constraints may be handled indirectly through penalty functions. A more direct way to incorporate constraints has been proposed by Fourman [12], who treats the structures in the population as lists of consistent constraints for VLSI layout problems.

Genetic algorithms have not enjoyed wide recognition, possibly due to a misconception that GA's are similar to early "evolutionary programming" techniques [11], which rely on random mutation and local hill-climbing. The basic concepts of GA's were developed by Holland [17] and his students [1], [2], [4], [6], [13], [15], [19]. These studies have produced the beginnings of a theory of genetic adaptive search. For example, an application of gambler's ruin theory to the allocation of trials to the hyperplanes of the search space shows that genetic techniques provide a near-optimal heuristic for information-gathering in complex search spaces [6], [17]. Bethke [1] provides theoretical characterizations of problems which may be especially well-suited or especially difficult for GA's [1]. In addition, a number of experimental studies show that GA's exhibit impressive efficiency in practice. While classical gradient search techniques are more efficient for problems which satisfy tight constraints, GA's consistently outperform both gradient techniques and various forms of random search on more difficult (and more common) problems, such as optimizations involving discontinuous, noisy, high-dimensional, and multimodal objective functions. GA's have been applied to various domains, including combinatorial optimization [12], [16], image processing [10], pipeline control systems [15], and machine learning [2], [18], [25].

III. Experimental Design

We now describe experiments which attempted to optimize the performance of GA's on a given set of function optimization problems. These experiments were designed to search the space of GA's defined by six control parameters, and to identify the optimal parameter settings with respect to two different performance measures. The searches for the optimal GA's were performed by GA's, which demonstrates the efficiency and power of GA's as metalevel optimization techniques. A metalevel GA could similarly search any other space of parameterized optimization procedures.

A. *The space of Genetic Algorithms*

Holland [17] describes a fairly general framework for the class of GA's. There are many possible elaborations of GA's involving variations such as other genetic operators, variable sized populations, etc. This study is limited to a particular subclass of GA's characterized by the following six parameters.

1) *Population Size* (N): The population size affects both the ultimate performance and the efficiency of GA's. GA's generally do poorly with very small populations [22], because the population provides an insufficient sample size for most hyperplanes. A large population is more likely to contain representatives from a large number of hyperplanes. Hence, the GA's can perform a more informed search. As a result, a large population discourages premature convergence to suboptimal solutions. On the other hand, a large population requires more evaluations per generation, possibly resulting in an unacceptably slow rate of convergence. In the current experiments, the population size ranged from 10 to 160 in increments of 10.

2) *Crossover Rate* (C): The crossover rate controls the frequency with which the crossover operator is applied. In each new population, $C * N$ structures undergo crossover. The higher the crossover rate, the more quickly new structures are introduced into the population. If the crossover rate is too high, high-performance structures are discarded faster than selection can produce improvements. If the crossover rate is too low, the search may stagnate due to the lower exploration rate. The current experiments allowed 16 different crossover rates, varying from 0.25 to 1.00 in increments of 0.05.

3) *Mutation Rate* (M): Mutation is a secondary search operator which increases the variability of the population. After selection, each bit position of each structure in the new population undergoes a random change with a probability equal to the mutation rate M. Consequently, approximately $M * N * L$ mutations occur per generation. A low level of mutation serves to prevent any given bit position from remaining forever converged to a single value in the entire population. A high level of mutation yields an essentially random search. The current experiments allowed eight values for the mutation rate, increasing exponentially from 0.0 to 1.0.

4) *Generation Gap* (G): The generation gap controls the percentage of the population to be replaced during each generation. That is $N * (1 - G)$ structures of $P(t)$ are chosen (at random) to survive intact in $P(t + 1)$. A value of $G = 1.0$ means that the entire population is replaced during each generation. A value of $G = 0.5$ means that half of the structures in each population survive into the next generation. The current experiments allowed G to vary between 0.30 and 1.00, in increments of 0.10.

5) *Scaling Window* (W): When maximizing a numerical function $f(x)$ with a GA, it is common to define the performance value $u(x)$ of a structure x as $u(x) = f(x) - f_{min}$, where f_{min} is the minimum value that $f(x)$ can assume in the given search space. This transformation guarantees that the performance U(x) is positive, regardless of the characteristics of $f(x)$. Often, f_{min} is not available *a priori*, in which case it is reasonable to define $u(x) = f(x) - f(x_{min})$, where $f(x_{min})$ is the minimum value of any structure evaluated so far. Either definition of $u(x)$ has the unfortunate effect of making good values of x hard to distinguish. For example, suppose $f_{min} = 0$. After several generations, the current population might contain only structures x for which $105 < f(x) < 110$. At this point, no structure in the population has a performance which deviates much from the average. This reduces the selection pressure toward the better structures, and the search stagnates. One solution is to define a new parameter f'_{min} with a value of say, 100, and rate each structure against this standard. For example, if $f(x_i) = 110$ and $f(x_j) = 105$, then $u(x_i) = f(x_i) - f'_{min} = 10$, and $u(x_j) = f(x_j) - f'_{min} = 5$; the performance of x_i now appears to be twice as good as the performance of x_j.

Our experiments investigated three scaling modes, based on a parameter called the scaling window W. If $W = 0$, then scaling was performed as follows: f'_{min} was set to the minimum $f(x)$ in the first generation. For each succeeding generation, those structures whose evaluations were less than f'_{min} were ignored in the selection procedure. The f'_{min} was updated whenever all the structures in a given population had evaluations greater than f'_{min}. If $0 < W < 7$, then we set f'_{min} to the least value of $f(x)$ which occurred in the last W generations. A value of $W = 7$ indicated an infinite window (i.e., no scaling was performed).

6) *Selection Strategy* (S): The experiments compared two selection strategies. If $S = P$, a *pure selection* procedure was used, in which each structure in the current population is reproduced a number of times proportional to the structure's performance. If $S = E$, an *elitist strategy* was employed. First, pure selection is performed. In addition, the elitist strategy stipulates that the structure with the best performance always survives intact into the next generation. In the absence of such a strategy, it is possible for the best structure to disappear, due to sampling error, crossover, or mutation.

We denote a particular GA by indicating its respective values for the parameters N, C, M, G, W, and S. Early work by De Jong [6] suggests parameter settings which have been used in a number of implementations of genetic algorithms. Based on De Jong's work, we define the *standard GA* as $GA_S = GA(50, 0.6, 0.001, 1.0, 7, E)$. The Cartesian product of the indicated ranges for the six parameters (N, C, M, G, W, S) defines a space of 2^{18} GA's. In some cases, it is possible to predict how variations of a single parameter will affect the performance of the GA's, assuming that all other parameters are kept fixed [6]. However, it is difficult to predict how the various parameters interact. For example, what is the effect of increasing the population size, while lowering the crossover rate? The analytic optimization of this space is well beyond our current understanding of GA's. It is also clear that an exhaustive enumeration of the space is infeasible. Our approach was to apply a metalevel GA's to the problem of identifying high-performance GA's. Each structure in the population of the metalevel GA consisted of an 18-bit vector which identified a particular GA. The performance of each GA was measured during the performance of a series of function optimization tasks. The metalevel GA used this information to conduct a search for high-performance algorithms.

B. *Task Environment*

Each GA was evaluated by using it to perform five optimization tasks, one for each of five carefully selected numerical test functions. As a result of these optimization tasks, the GA was assigned a value according to one of the performance measures explained below. The functions comprising the task environment have been studied in previous studies of GA's [3], [6] and included functions with various characteristics, including discontinuous, multidimensional, and noisy functions. Table I gives a brief description of the test functions.

C. *Performance Measures*

Two performance metrics for adaptive search strategies were considered, *on-line performance* and *off-line performance* [6]. The on-line performance of a search strategy s on a response surface e is defined as follows:

$$U_e(s, T) = \text{ave}_t(u_e(t)), \qquad t = 0, 1, \cdots, T$$

where $u_e(t)$ is the performance of the structure evaluated at time t. That is, on-line performance is the average performance of all tested structures over the course of the search.

The off-line performance of a search strategy s on a response surface e is defined as follows:

$$U_e^*(s, T) = \text{ave}_t(u_e^*(t)), \qquad t = 0, 1, \cdots, T$$

where $u_e^*(t)$ is the best performance achieved in the time interval $[0, t]$. Off-line performance is the relevant measure when the search can be performed off-line (e.g., via a simulation model), while the best structure so far is used to control the on-line system.

In order to measure global robustness, corresponding performance measures are defined for the entire set of response surfaces E:

$$U_E(s, T) = 100.0 * \text{ave}_e(U_e(s, T)/U_e(\text{rand}, T)),$$
$$e \text{ in } E$$

$$U_E^*(s, T) = 1000 * \text{ave}_e(U_e^*(s, T)/U_e^*(\text{rand}, T)),$$
$$e \text{ in } E$$

TABLE I
FUNCTIONS COMPRISING THE TEST ENVIRONMENT

Function	Dimensions	Size of Space	Description
$f1$	3	1.0×10^9	parabola
$f2$	2	1.7×10^6	Rosenbrock's saddle [23]
$f3$	5	1.0×10^{15}	step function
$f4$	30	1.0×10^{72}	quartic with noise
$f5$	2	1.6×10^{10}	Shekel's foxholes [24]

where $U_e(\text{rand}, T)$ and $U_e^*(\text{rand}, T)$ are on-line and off-line performance, respectively, of pure random search on response surface E. As normalized, U_E and U_E^* for random search will be 100.0, while U_e and U_E^* for more effective search strategies will be correspondingly lower (for minimization problems).

D. *Experimental Procedures*

Two experiments were performed, one to optimize on-line performance and one to optimize off-line performance. For each experiment, the procedure for obtaining the optimum GA was as follows.

1) One thousand GA's were evaluated, using a metalevel GA to perform the search through the space of GA's defined by the six GA parameters. Each evaluation comprised running one GA against each of the five test functions for 5000 function evaluations and normalizing the result with respect to the performance of random search on the same function. The metalevel GA started with a population of 50 randomly chosen GA's and used the standard parameter settings, i.e., GA (50, 0.6, 0.001, 1.0, 7, E). Past experience has shown that these parameters yield a fairly good search for a variety of problems, and so this was the natural choice for the metalevel.

2) Since GA's are randomized algorithms, the performance of a GA during a single trial in the metalevel experiment represents a sample from a distribution of performances. Therefore, it was decided that the GA's showing the best performances during step 1 would be subjected to more extensive testing. Each of the 20 best GA's in step 1 was again run against the task environment, this time for five trials for each test function, using different random number seeds for each trial. The GA which exhibited the best performance in this step was declared the winner of the experiment.

IV. RESULTS

A. *Experiment I—Online Performance*

The first experiment was designed to search for the optimal GA with respect to on-line performance on the task environment. Fig. 4 shows the average online performance for the 50 GA's in each of the 20 generations of experiment 1. Recall that the overall scores for random search on the task environment is 100.0. From the initial data point in Fig. 4, we can estimate that the average on-line performance of all GA's in our search space is approximately 56.6,

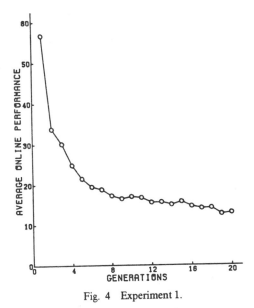

Fig. 4 Experiment 1.

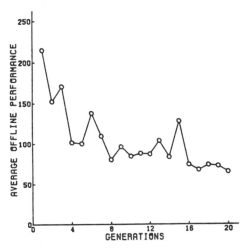

Fig. 5 Experiment 2.

or about 43.4 percent better than random search. Fig. 4 shows that the final population of GA's had significantly better performance than the average GA.

This experiment identified $GA_1 = GA(30, 0.95, 0.01, 1.0, 1, E)$ as the optimal GA with respect to on-line performance. In an extended comparison, GA_1 showed a 3.09 percent improvement (with respect to the baseline performance of random search) over GA_s on the task environment. This represents a small but statistically significant improvement over the expected on-line performance of GA_s. The performance improvement between GA_s and GA_1 can be attributed to an interaction among a number of factors. First, GA_1 uses a smaller population, which allows many more generations within a given number of trials. For example, on functions in the task environment, GA_1 iterated through an average of twice as many generations as GA_s. Second, GA_s uses an infinite window, i.e., no scaling is performed. GA_1 uses a small window (one generation), which resulted in a more directed search. These two factors are apparently balanced by the significantly increased crossover rate and mutation rate in GA_1. A higher crossover rate tends to disrupt the structures selected for reproduction at a high rate, which is important in a small population, since high performance individuals are more likely to quickly dominate the population. The higher mutation rate also helps prevent premature convergence to local optima.

B. *Experiment 2—Off-line Performance*

The second experiment was designed to search for the optimal GA with respect to off-line performance on the task environment. Fig. 5 shows that the average off-line performance of all GA's (214.8) appears to be much worse than the average off-line performance of random search (100.0). This finding verifies the experience of many practitioners that GA's can prematurely converge to suboptimal solutions when given the wrong control parameters. For example, if a very small population size is used (i.e., N = 10), the number of representatives from any given hyperplane is so small that the selection procedure has insufficient information

to properly apportion credit to the hyperplanes represented in the population. As a result, a relatively good structure may overrun the entire population in a few generations. Unless the mutation rate is high, the GA will quickly converge to a suboptimal solution. In contrast, random search will usually locate at least one high performance point within the first thousand trials, leading to relatively good off-line performance. That is, random search is a fairly tough competitor for search strategies when the goal is good off-line performance. It is encouraging that many GA's perform significantly better than random search with respect to the off-line performance measure.

This experiment identified $GA_2 = GA(80, 0.45, 0.01, 0.9, 1, P)$ as the optimal GA with respect to off-line performance. In an extended comparison, GA_2 showed a 3.0 percent performance improvement over GA_s on the task environment. Because of the high variance shown by GA's with respect to off-line performance, this does not represent a statistically significant difference between GA_2 and GA_s. There are several interesting differences between GA_2 and GA_s. With a larger population and higher mutation rate, the population will tend to contain more variety, thus increasing the random aspects of the GA. The slightly lower generation gap also tends to reduce the effects of selection, resulting in a less focused search. These aspects are balanced by the lower crossover rate and the small scaling window which tend to enhance the selective pressure.

C. General Observations

Besides suggesting optimal GA's, the above experiments also provide performance data for 2000 GA's with various parameter settings. Given that these are not independent samples from the space of GA's, it is rather difficult to make valid statistical inferences from this data. Nevertheless the data does suggest some regularities that might warrant further studies.

The experimental data confirms several observations first made by De Jong on the basis of a relatively small number of experiments [6]. For example, mutation rates above 0.05 are generally harmful with respect to on-line

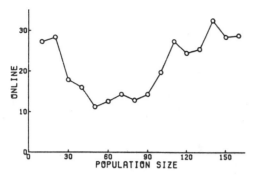

Fig. 6 Average online performance of various population sizes according to Experiment 1.

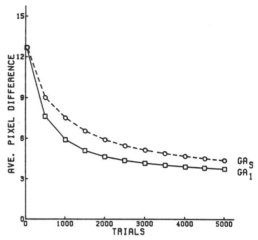

Fig. 7 Online performance of GA_1 and GA_S on an image registration task.

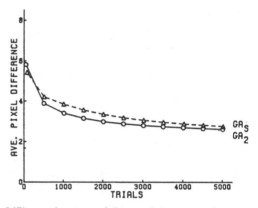

Fig. 8 Offline performance of GA_2 and GA_S on an image registration task.

performance, with performance approaching that of random search with rates above 0.1 regardless of the other parameter settings. The absence of mutation is also associated with poorer performance, which suggests that mutation performs an important service in refreshing lost values. Best on-line performance can be obtained with a population size in the range of 30-100 structures as shown by Fig. 6, which plots the average on-line performance as a function of population size, ignoring those GA's with mutation rates above 0.05.

A similar graph can be obtained for off-line performance except that range for the best population size is 60-110 structures. A large generation gap generally improves performance, as does the elitist selection strategy.

The performance data also suggests other regularities that have not been previously noted. First, the adoption of a small window (1-5 generations) is associated with a slight improvement in both on-line and off-line performance. This is reasonable since scaling enhances the pressure of selection in later stages of the search. In small populations (20 to 40 structures), good on-line performance is associated with either a high crossover rate combined with a low mutation rate or a low crossover rate combined with a high mutation rate. For mid-sized populations (30 to 90 structures), the optimal crossover rate appears to decrease as the population size increases. For example, among the best 10 percent of all GA's with population size 30, the average crossover rate was 0.88. The best crossover rate decreases to 0.50 for population size 50 and to 0.30 for population size 80. This is reasonable since, in smaller populations, crossover plays an important role in preventing premature convergence. In summary, the performance of GA's appear to be a nonlinear function of the control parameters. However, the available data is too limited to confirm or disconfirm the existence of discontinuities or multiple local optima in the performance space of GA's. It would be interesting to compare the performance of other nonlinear search techniques in optimizing the performance of GA's.

V. VALIDATION

In order to validate the experimental results, the three algorithms GA_s, GA_1 and GA_2 were applied to an optimization problem which was not included in the experimental

task environment. The validation task was the following image registration problem: In order to compare two gray-level images of a scene taken at different times or from different vantage points, it is often necessary to determine a transformation, or *registration*, which will map one image, the original image, into another, the target image. This registration problem is important in such diverse fields as aerial photography and medical imaging [20], [21]. One approach to the image registration problem [10] is to define a parameterized class of transformations and to apply a GA to the task of searching this class for an optimal transformation, i.e., a transformation which maps the original image into the target image. The response surface for a given pair of images is a function of the transformation and corresponds to the average gray-level differences between corresponding pixels in the transformed original image and the target image. This class of problems appears to be difficult for conventional nonlinear programming algorithms due to the inevitable presence of many local minima [14].

Experiments were conducted to compare the effectiveness of the algorithms GA_s, GA_1, and GA_2 for a sample registration problem consisting of a pair of carotid artery images in which patient motion produced significant motion artifacts. Each experiment consisted of five runs of a GA on the pair of images, each run evaluating 5000 candidate transformations. Fig. 7 compares the on-line performance of GA_s with GA_1. GA_1 shows a small but statistically significant improvement in on-line performance over GA_s on this problem. Fig. 8 shows that GA_2 produces no significant difference in off-line performance over GA_s. These results are consistent with the results in Experiments 1 and 2, and indicate that those results may be generally applicable to other optimization problems.

VI. CONCLUSION

Experiments were performed to search for the optimal GA's for a given set of numerical optimization problems. Previous experiments show that the standard GA, GA_s, outperforms several classical optimization techniques on the task environment. Thus, one goal of our experiments was to identify GA's which are at least as good as GA_s. Both experiments succeeded in identifying control parameters settings that optimize GA's with respect to the described performance metrics. The experimental data also suggests that, while it is possible to optimize GA control parameters, very good performance can be obtained with a range of GA control parameter settings.

The present approach is limited in several ways. First, it was necessary to choose a particular parameterized subclass of GA's to explore. In particular, we have neglected other recombination operators such as multipoint crossover and inversion and other strategies such as the inclusion of a "crowding factor" [6]. Second, the GA's we considered were essentially unconstrained optimization procedures. As previously noted, there are ways to incorporate constraints into GA's but it remains for future research to determine how the presence of constraints affects the optimal control parameters. Finally, the metalevel experiments represent a sizable number of CPU hours. It is encouraging that the results appear to be applicable to a wide class of optimization problems.

An alternative approach to the optimization of GA's would enable the GA to modify its own parameters dynamically during the search. However, for many optimization problems the number of evaluations which can be performed in a reasonable amount of time would not allow the GA enough evaluations to modify its search techniques to any significant degree. Therefore, the experiments described above are important in that they identify approximately optimal parameter settings for the two performance measures considered. The data also suggests several new tradeoffs among the control parameters which may lead to further theoretical insights concerning the behavior of genetic algorithms.

REFERENCES

[1] A.D. Bethke, "Genetic algorithms as function optimizers," Ph.D. thesis, Dept. Computer and Communication Sciences, Univ. of Michigan, 1981.

[2] L.B. Booker, "Intelligent behavior as an adaptation to the task of environment," Ph.D. thesis, Dept. Computer and Communication Sciences, Univ. of Michigan, Feb. 1982.

[3] A. Brindle, "Genetic algorithms, for functional optimization," Ph.D. thesis, Computer Sciences Dept., Univ. of Alberta, 1981.

[4] D.J. Cavicchio, "Adaptive search using simulated evolution," Ph.D. thesis, Dept. Computer and Communication Sciences, Univ. of Michigan, 1970.

[5] L.Cooper and D. Steinberg, *Methods of Optimization*, Philadelphia: W.B. Saunders, 1970.

[6] K.A. DeJong, "Analysis of the behavior of a class of genetic adaptive systems," Ph.D. thesis, Dept. Computer and Communication Sciences, Univ. of Michigan, 1975.

[7] —, "Adaptive system design: A genetic approach," *IEEE Trans. Syst., Man, Cyber.*, Vol. SMC-10, No. 9, pp. 566-574, Sept. 1980

[8] L.C.W. Dixon, "The choice of step length, a crucial factor in the performance of variable metric algorithms," in *Numerical Methods for Nonlinear Optimization*, F.A. Lootsma, Ed., New York: Academic Press, 1972.

[9] W. Farrel, *Optimization Techniques for Computerized Simulation*, Los Angeles: CACI, 1975.

[10] J.M. Fitzpatrick, J.J. Grefenstette, and D. Van Gucht, "Image registration by genetic search," in *Proc. of IEEE Southeastcon '84*, pp. 460-464, April 1984.

[11] L.J. Fogel, A.J. Owens, and M.J. Walsh, *Artificial Intelligence Through Simulated Evolution*, New York: Wiley and Sons, 1966.

[12] M.P. Fourman, "Compaction of symbolic layout using genetic algorithms," *Proc. Intl. Conf. on Genetic Algorithms and their Applications*, pp. 141-153, July 1985.

[13] D.R. Frantz, "Non-linearities in genetic adaptive search," Ph.D. thesis, Dept. Computer and Communication Sciences, Univ. of Michigan, 1972.

[14] W. Frei, T. Shibata, and C.C. Chen, "Fast matching of non-stationary images with false fix protection," *Proc. 5th Intl. Conf. Patt. Recog.*, Vol. 1, IEEE, 1980, pp. 208-212.

[15] D. Goldberg, "Computer-aided gas pipeline operation using genetic algorithms and rule learning," Ph.D. thesis., Dept. Civil Eng., Univ. of Michigan, 1983.

[16] J.J. Grefenstette, R. Gopal, B.J. Rosmaita, and D. Van Gucht, "Genetic algorithms for the traveling salesman problem," in *Proc. Int. Conf. Genetic Algorithms and their Applications*, pp. 160-168, July 1985.

[17] J.H. Holland, *Adaptation in Natural and Artificial Systems*, Univ. of Michigan, Ann Arbor, MI, 1975.

[18] —, "Escaping brittleness," in *Proc. Int. Machine Learning Workshop*, pp. 92-95, June 1983.

[19] R.B. Hollstien, "Artificial Genetic Adaptation in Computer Control Systems," Ph.D. thesis, Computer and Communication Sciences, Univ. of Michigan, 1971.

[20] R.A. Kruger and S.J. Riederer, *Basic Concepts of Digital Subtraction Angiography*, Boston: G.K. Hall, 1984.

[21] James J. Little, "Automatic registration of landsat MSS images to digital elevation models," in *Proc. IEEE Workshop Computer Vision: Representation and Control*, pp. 178-184, 1982.

[22] E. Pettit and K.M. Swigger, "An analysis of genetic-based pattern tracking," in *Proc. National Conf. on AI, AAAI '83*, pp. 327-332, 1983.

[23] H.H. Rosenbrock, "An automatic method for finding the greatest or least value of a function," *Computer J.*, Vol. 3, Oct. 1960, pp. 175-184.

[24] J. Shekel, "Test functions for multimodal search techniques," in *Fifth Ann. Princeton Conf. Inform. Sci. Syst.*, 1971.

[25] S.F. Smith, "Flexible learning of problem solving heuristics through adaptive search," in *Proc. of 8th IJCAI*, 1983.

How Genetic Algorithms Work:
A Critical Look at Implicit Parallelism

John J. Grefenstette
Naval Research Laboratory
Washington, DC 20375-5000

James E. Baker
Bell Laboratories
Whippany, NJ 07981

ABSTRACT

The power of a genetic algorithm derives largely from its *implicit parallelism*, i.e., the simultaneous allocation of search effort to many regions of the search space according to sound principles. In this paper, we examine how well currently available theoretical results describe the actual search behavior of genetic algorithms as used in practice, and offer suggestions for improving the applicability of the theory.

1. INTRODUCTION

Since Holland's seminal work (Holland, 1975), there has been a growing number of applications of genetic algorithms to a variety of optimization and learning tasks. These implementations often have fundamental differences, and as a result, it is difficult to provide a theoretical characterization of the search behavior that one might expect from a genetic algorithm. This paper examines how well the Schema Theorem (Holland, 1975) describes the actual behavior of genetic algorithms. We argue that the Schema Theorem requires additional interpretation before it can be applied to many successful implementations of genetic algorithms. We present a few alternatives that may provide a more useful basis for characterizing the behavior of various classes of genetic algorithms. We summarize extensive empirical studies that show that a number of different genetic algorithms exhibit comparable search performance on a variety of optimization problems.

We adopt the following outline of a genetic algorithm:

```
procedure GA
begin
    t = 0;
    initialize P(t);
    evaluate structures in P(t);
    while termination condition not satisfied do
    begin
        t = t + 1;
        select P(t) from P(t−1);
        recombine structures in P(t);
        evaluate structures in P(t);
    end
end.
```

Fig. 1. A Genetic Algorithm

The population $P(t)$ is assumed to be of constant size, N. The *initialization* is assumed to be random. *Recombination* typically involves crossover and mutation and perhaps other genetic operators. While the study of recombination operators is obviously important in its own right, it is traditional to characterize the effects of recombination in terms of the disruption to the allocation of trials to hyperplanes that results from the selection phase. In this paper, we restrict our attention to the selection phase, and leave the analysis of various recombination operators for another time.

The goal of this paper is to describe how genetic algorithms work, in terms of interest to someone who has a particular optimization problem in mind. By focusing on genetic algorithms as optimization procedures, we do not mean to imply any restriction on form of the function to be optimized, but only that the external problem presents a well-defined measure of the behavior of candidate solution

2. SELECTION ALGORITHMS

It is convenient to partition the selection phase into two distinct algorithms: the selection algorithm and the sampling algorithm. The *selection algorithm* assigns to each individual x a real number we call its *target sampling rate*, $tsr(x,t)$, that indicates the expected number of offspring to be generated from that individual at time t. The *sampling algorithm* produces a new population by creating copies of individuals based on the target sampling rates. The sampling algorithm should be designed with care, since it necessarily introduces stochastic effects as it maps from an individual's real-valued *tsr* to an integer number of copies of that individual. Baker (1987) has described an optimal sampling algorithm, which we assume is used in the genetic algorithms under discussion. Hence, in this paper, we are free to focus on the selection algorithm, i.e., the rule for computing the *tsr* of each individual. Of particular interest is the effect of different selection algorithms on the allocation of trials to hyperplanes. For any selection algorithm, the allocation of trials to individuals induces a corresponding allocation to hyperplanes represented by the individuals:

$$tsr(H,t) =_{def} \sum_{i=1}^{m(H,t)} \frac{tsr(x_i,t)}{m(H,t)}$$

where $x_i \in H$ and $m(H,t)$ denotes the number of

representatives of hyperplane H in population $P(t)$. We will often refer to $tsr(H,t)$ as the *growth rate* of H at time t, and neglect the disruption caused by recombination operators.

Many reasonable selection algorithms are possible. Certainly the most widely known technique is *proportional selection*:

$$tsr(x,t) = \frac{u(x)}{\bar{u}(t)} \qquad (1)$$

where u is the *fitness function* and $\bar{u}(t)$ denotes the average fitness of the individuals in $P(t)$. The most attractive feature of proportional selection is that it induces the following target sampling rates for all hyperplanes in the population:

$$tsr(H,t) = \sum_{i=1}^{m(H,t)} \frac{tsr(x_i,t)}{m(H,t)}$$

$$= \sum_{i=1}^{m(H,t)} \frac{u(x_i)}{\bar{u}(t)\,m(H,t)}$$

$$= \frac{u(H,t)}{\bar{u}(t)} \qquad (2)$$

where $u(H,t)$ is simply the average fitness of the representatives of H in $P(t)$. This result is the heart of the Schema Theorem (Holland, 1975), which has been called the Fundamental Theorem of Genetic Algorithms (Goldberg, 1989):

Schema Theorem (Holland, 1975). In a genetic algorithm using a proportional selection algorithm and (single-point) crossover, the following holds for each hyperplane H represented in $P(t)$:

$$M(H,t+1) \geq M(H,t)(\frac{u(H,t)}{\bar{u}(t)})(1 - \frac{p_c d(H)}{L-1})$$

where $M(H,t)$ is the expected number of representatives of hyperplane H in $P(t)$, p_c is the crossover rate, $d(H)$ is the defining length of hyperplane H, and L is the length of each individual.

The Schema Theorem can be sharpened by adding additional terms indicating the disruptive effect of mutation and other operators (Bridges & Goldberg, 1987), but its main thrust is that trials are allocated *in parallel* to a large number of hyperplanes (i.e., the ones with short definition lengths) according to the sampling rate in (1), with minor disruption from the recombination operators. As a result, the number of trials allocated to any short definition length hyperplane with persistently above average fitness grows at an exponential rate, while trials to those with below average fitness rapidly decline in numbers.

An alternative to proportional selection is *linear rank selection*:

$$tsr(x,t) = Min + (Max - Min)\frac{rank(x,t) - 1}{N - 1} \qquad (3)$$

where $rank(x,t)$ is the index of x when $P(t)$ is sorted in increasing order by $u(x)$. That is, the worst individual is assigned a *tsr* of *Min*, the best is assigned a *tsr* of *Max*, and the *tsr* for each of the other individuals is interpolated according to its rank.[1] The primary advantage of ranking over proportional selection is that the resulting algorithm is less prone to premature convergence caused by individuals that are far above average. (And, one might argue, selection by ranking seems closer to the mechanism of natural selection.) A number of other alternative selection algorithms have also been studied (Whitley, 1987; Goldberg, 1989; Baker, 1989), but have not enjoyed the same level of theoretical analysis as the proportional selection algorithm. The following analysis was motivated in part by a desire to fill this theoretical void.

3. THE IMPACT OF THE FITNESS FUNCTION

Proportional selection and linear rank selection each define an infinite class of selection algorithms, depending on the choice of the fitness function u. In general, the fitness function consists of the composition of two functions (De Jong, 1975):

$$u(x) = g(f(x)),$$

where f is the objective function and g transforms the value of the objective function to a non-negative number. The mapping performed by g is always necessary when the objective function is to be minimized (since lower objective function values must map to higher fitness values) or when the objective function can take on negative values. The fitness function u is often a linear transformation of the objective function:

$$u(x) = a f(x) + b \qquad (4)$$

where a is positive if we are maximizing f and negative if we are minimizing, and b is selected to ensure non-negative fitness.

In his early discussion of genetic algorithms, Holland implicitly assumes a non-negative fitness and he does not address the problem of mapping from objective function to fitness in his brief discussion of function optimization (Holland, 1975; Ch. 3). Unfortunately, the absence of a canonical fitness function makes interpretation of the Schema Theorem problematical. For example, consider two genetic algorithms that both use proportional selection but that differ in that one uses the fitness function

$$u_1(x) = a f(x) + b$$

and the other uses the fitness function

---

[1] The constraints that $0 \leq tsr(x,t)$ and $\sum tsr(x,t) = N$ require that $1 \leq Max \leq 2$ and $Min = 2 - Max$.

$$u_2(x) = a f(x) + b + c, \quad c \neq 0.$$

Then for any short definition length hyperplane H represented in a given population $P(t)$, the growth rate for H in the first algorithm is

$$tsr_1(H,t) = \frac{u_1(H,t)}{\bar{u}_1(t)}$$

while the growth rate for H in the second algorithm is

$$tsr_2(H,t) = \frac{u_2(H,t)}{\bar{u}_2(t)}$$

$$= \frac{u_1(H,t) + c}{\bar{u}_1(t) + c}.$$

Even though both genetic algorithms behave according to the Schema Theorem, they clearly allocate trials to hyperplanes at different rates. It follows that the Schema Theorem does not prescribe a unique allocation of trials for a given optimization problem.

The interpretation of the Schema Theorem becomes even less clear if the fitness function u is dynamically scaled during the course of the algorithm. The motivation for dynamic scaling is that the genetic algorithm quickly evolves a population of high-performance structures. That is, the values of $f(x)$ tend to converge to a narrow range. If a constant transformation like (4) is adopted for the fitness function, then selective pressure rapidly declines as the individuals in the population converge to relatively equal levels of fitness. Many forms of dynamic fitness scaling have been suggested (Grefenstette, 1986; Goldberg, 1989). For example, a *dynamic linear fitness function* has the form

$$u(x) = a f(x) + b(t). \tag{5}$$

where $b(t)$ provides the scaling effect. One possible definition for $b(t)$ is

$$b(t) = -\min \{f(x) \mid x \in P(t)\}$$

(assuming we are maximizing $f(x)$), in effect raising the standard against which fitness is measured, and thereby maintaining a strong selective pressure throughout the course of the search.[2] If the fitness function changes adaptively, it is difficult to say what constraints the Schema Theorem places on the allocation of trials to hyperplanes.

The problem is that the Schema Theorem is not sufficiently grounded in the external problem. That is, it refers to the *fitness* function rather than the *objective* function, and the fitness function should be considered a design parameter of the genetic algorithm, not a feature of the optimization problem. It would be more useful to have theorems that tell us how the space *defined by the objective*

function is searched by genetic algorithms with particular design parameters (e.g., fitness mapping, selection algorithm, recombination operators, etc.). The remainder of the paper presents some efforts in that direction.

First, let's restate the thrust of the Schema Theorem in terms of the objective function. Let $\Theta(t)$ denote the set of all hyperplanes in a given population:

$$\Theta(t) = \{H_i \mid H_i \text{ is represented in } P(t)\}.$$

We say that Π_t is a *canonical ordering of* $\Theta(t)$ if Π_t is a permutation of $\{1, 2, \cdots, |\Theta(t)|\}$ such that for any pair H_i, H_j in $\Theta(t)$,

$$\Pi_t(i) < \Pi_t(j) \rightarrow \alpha f(H_i,t) \leq \alpha f(H_j,t)$$

where $f(H_i,t)$ is the average value of the objective function over the representatives of H_i in $P(t)$ and $\alpha = 1$ if we are maximizing f and $\alpha = -1$ if we are minimizing f. That is, Π_t is simply a sorting of the hyperplanes in $P(t)$ in order of increasing performance.[3] These definitions enable us to characterize the behavior of a large class of genetic algorithms in terms of the objective function.

Theorem 1. In any genetic algorithm using a proportional selection algorithm (1) and a dynamic linear fitness function (5), for any pair of hyperplanes H_i, H_j in $P(t)$,

$$\Pi_t(i) < \Pi_t(j) \rightarrow tsr(H_i,t) \leq tsr(H_j,t). \tag{6}$$

Proof. Without loss of generality, assume that we are maximizing over f. Consider two hyperplanes H_i and H_j such that $\Pi_t(i) < \Pi_t(j)$. That is, $f(H_i,t) \leq f(H_j,t)$. Since the fitness function is linear, $f(H_i,t) \leq f(H_j,t)$ implies that $u(H_i,t) \leq u(H_j,t)$. Under the proportional selection regime, the growth rate of each hyperplane is $tsr(H,t) = u(H,t) / \bar{u}(t)$, so $u(H_i,t) \leq u(H_j,t)$ implies that $tsr(H_i,t) \leq tsr(H_j,t)$. $\square$

Theorem 1 captures much of what is commonly meant by the *implicit parallelism* of genetic algorithms. In particular, we have the following:

Corollary 1. In any genetic algorithm using a proportional selection algorithm and a dynamic linear fitness function, for any two short definition length hyperplanes H_i and H_j, such that the observed performance of H_i is consistently higher than the observed performance of H_j, H_i grows at an exponentially greater rate than H_j.

Of course, Corollary 1 does not specify exactly which exponential function describes the relative growth rate of any two hyperplanes, since the exact growth rates depend on the scaling of the fitness function. However, both Theorem 1 and Corollary 1 are invariant under dynamic linear scaling of the fitness function, and so they are more explicitly descriptive of genetic algorithms in widespread use than is

---

[2] In practice, $b(t)$ should change rather smoothly to provide a more stable fitness function.

[3] Canonical orderings are not unique since hyperplanes with equal performance can be in any order.

the original Schema Theorem.

Unfortunately, Theorem 1 can not be extended to some other reasonable fitness functions. For example, in some early experiments on their image registration project, Fitzpatrick and Grefenstette (1983) used the following fitness mapping for minimizing an objective function f that was known to be everywhere positive:

$$u(x) = b - \log(f(x)) \qquad (7)$$

where b was chosen to be larger than any value of $\log(f(x))$. This logarithmic mapping has two desirable effects. First, it minimizes the danger of premature convergence by damping out differences in the early stages when all individuals have rather large values of $f(x)$. Second, it exaggerates small differences as $f(x)$ approaches 0. Although this seems to be a reasonable fitness mapping for the given problem, the resulting genetic algorithm does not satisfy (6). Here is a simple counterexample. Suppose that $b = 10$ and $N = 4$. Furthermore, suppose that the hyperplane $H_0 = 0\#\cdots\#$ is represented in $P(t)$ by the individuals x_1 and x_2, where $f(x_1) = 1$ and $f(x_2) = 256$. Then

$$u(x_1) = 10 - \log(1) = 10 \text{ and}$$

$$u(x_2) = 10 - \log(256) = 2, \text{ so}$$

$$u(H_0, t) = 6.$$

Now suppose that the hyperplane $H_1 = 1\#\cdots\#$ is represented in $P(t)$ by the individuals x_3 and x_4, where $f(x_3) = f(x_4) = 64$. Then

$$u(x_3) = u(x_4) = 10 - \log(64) = 4, \text{ so}$$

$$u(H_1, t) = 4.$$

The average fitness for the entire population is then $\bar{u}(t) = 5$, so the growth rates for the hyperplanes are:

$$tsr(H_0, t) = \frac{u(H_0, t)}{\bar{u}(t)} = 1.2, \text{ and}$$

$$tsr(H_1, t) = \frac{u(H_1, t)}{\bar{u}(t)} = 0.8.$$

So even though $f(H_1, t) = 64 < f(H_0, t) = 128.5$ and we are minimizing f, H_0 has a higher growth rate than H_1.

The problem with this fitness function with respect to Theorem 1 is that, by taking the logarithm of the the objective function values, the average fitness of a hyperplane no longer necessarily reflects the average observed performance, as measured by the objective function. It follows that the conditions of Theorem 1 can not be weakened to cover logarithmic scaling methods. Similar remarks apply to scaling methods using power laws (Gillies, 1985):

$$u(x) = (af(x) + b)^k \qquad (8)$$

where a and b are chosen as in linear scaling methods.

It may seem tempting to restrict fitness scaling methods to linear transformations in order to satisfy Corollary 1. On the other hand, perhaps the behavior described by Corollary 1 is more restrictive than necessary for a successful genetic algorithm. Let's examine the reasons for wanting Corollary 1 in the first place.

4. THE K-ARMED BANDITS ANALOGY

Much of the motivation for Corollary 1 comes from Holland's detailed analysis of the k-armed bandit problem, which we summarize as follows: Given a number of competing payoff sources with unknown rates of payoff, a nearly optimal adaptive strategy is to allocate an exponentially increasing number of trials to the one with the observed best performance. Holland shows that this strategy achieves a balance between the conflicting goals of exploiting the current payoff estimates and improving the payoff estimates in order to avoid irrevocable incorrect decisions.

It is often claimed that the power of a genetic algorithm arises from solving a large number of such problems in parallel, where the sources of payoff are the short definition length hyperplanes (Goldberg, 1989). It is clear that (6) does result in an exponential increase in trials allocated to a hyperplane whose observed average fitness is consistently above its competing hyperplanes. Thus, it is tempting to say that the genetic algorithm identifies high performance, short definition length hyperplanes by Holland's k-armed bandit strategy, and these hyperplanes then serve as building blocks for further exploration.

While Holland's analysis of the k-armed bandit problem seems correct, its application to the way genetic algorithms allocate trials to hyperplanes is unclear. Consider the following case: Suppose that

$$u(x) = 2 \text{ if } x \in 111\#\cdots\#$$

$$u(x) = 1 \text{ if } x \in 0\#\#\#\cdots\#$$

$$u(x) = 0 \text{ otherwise.}$$

Now suppose that the initial population is uniformly distributed across the search space, and that the genetic algorithm uses a proportional selection algorithm. Using (2), we can predict the allocation of trials over the first few generations, as shown in Table 1. At time $t = 0$, the genetic algorithm obtains an accurate estimate of the relative payoff rates of the two hyperplanes $0\#\cdots\#$ and $1\#\cdots\#$, and allocates trials accordingly at $t = 1$. But these trials are not allocated uniformly across $1\#\cdots\#$. They are allocated entirely to the subspace $111\#\cdots\#$.[4] This set of trials results in a higher observed estimate for the fitness of $1\#\cdots\#$, leading to a domination in the population by this hyperplane

---

[4] We are assuming that the length of the individuals is large, say $L > 100$, so that we may ignore the disruptive effects of crossover on these short definition length hyperplanes.

Representatives in Population					
t	0	1	2	3	4
0### $\cdots$ #	N/2	2N/3	N/2	N/3	N/5
1### $\cdots$ #	N/2	N/3	N/2	2N/3	4N/5
111# $\cdots$ #	N/8	N/3	N/2	2N/3	4N/5
$\bar{u}(t)$	3/4	4/3	3/2	5/3	9/5

Table 1. Allocation of trials to competing hyperplanes.

from $t = 3$ onward. Of course, the true average fitnesses are

$$u(0\# \cdots \#) = 1, \text{ and}$$

$$u(1\# \cdots \#) = 1/2.$$

It seems strange to say that the genetic algorithm has solved a 2-armed bandit problem involving the hyperplane partition defined by $0\# \cdots \#$ and $1\# \cdots \#$, since it ends up allocating the majority of trials to the "arm" with the lesser average payoff. The analogy with the 2-armed bandit problem breaks down because the genetic algorithm does not perform uniform sampling from the hyperplanes in the population, at least not after the initial generation. A careful reading of Holland's original analysis shows that the optimal adaptive strategy for 2-armed bandit problems depends on the assumption that *additional trials provide additional evidence for estimating the true payoff rates*. Unlike a player of 2-armed bandits, the genetic algorithm does not take unbiased samples from the hyperplanes represented in the population, and so does not treat the competition between $0\# \cdots \#$ and $1\# \cdots \#$ as a 2-armed bandit problem.

Putting this in general terms, the theoretical support for an exponential allocation of trials to the observed best one of a set of competing hyperplanes rests on an analogy between the hyperplane competition and the k-armed bandits problem. The analogy is strongest when the hyperplanes involved exhibit little variance in their fitness, and is weakest when the hyperplanes have high fitness variance (like $1\# \cdots \#$ above). In the case of a high variance hyperplane, the genetic algorithm performs a highly biased sampling of the hyperplane, biased toward its high performance subspaces. In summary, there seems to be little motivation for a strict requirement that all hyperplanes satisfy (6). The genetic algorithm seems to adaptively select the level at which to apply the optimal k-armed bandit strategy, rather than applying it to hyperplane partitions at all levels. We conjecture that the k-armed bandit problems to which the genetic algorithm applies Holland's adaptive strategy are those hyperplane partitions whose hyperplanes exhibit very little variance in their fitness functions. If this

conjecture is true, then perhaps our theory should focus on such hyperplanes. The next section develops the beginning of such a theory.

5. ANOTHER VIEW OF IMPLICIT PARALLELISM

By dropping the requirement that all hyperplane competitions satisfy (6), it is possible to characterize the behavior of a fairly broad class of genetic algorithms. We first need a few more definitions. We say that u is a *monotonic fitness function* if the following condition holds:

$$u(x_i) \leq u(x_j) \text{ iff } \alpha f(x_i) \leq \alpha f(x_j) \qquad (9)$$

where $\alpha = 1$ if we are maximizing f and $\alpha = -1$ if we are minimizing f. The class of monotonic fitness functions includes dynamic linear scaling functions (5), as well as logarithmic (7) and power scaling functions (8). Furthermore, we say that a *monotonic selection algorithm* is one that assigns a target sampling rate to individuals such that:

$$tsr(x_i) \leq tsr(x_j) \text{ iff } u(x_i) \leq u(x_j). \qquad (10)$$

The class of monotonic selection algorithms includes proportional selection (1), selection by ranking (3), and just about any other selection algorithm that does not violate the idea of reproduction according to fitness. Thus, the class of genetic algorithms that use monotonic fitness functions and monotonic selection algorithms includes not only all of the successful genetic algorithms implemented to date, but also many with possibly degenerate search behavior, such as an algorithm that assigns every individual a *tsr* of 1. Nevertheless, it is interesting to see what we can say about the behavior of this class of genetic algorithms. For this we need one more definition. We say that hyperplane H_i *is dominated by* H_j *in* $P(t)$ ($H_i \leq_{D,t} H_j$) if

$$\max \{\alpha f(x) \mid x \in H_i \cap P(t)\} \leq \qquad (11)$$

$$\min \{\alpha f(x) \mid x \in H_j \cap P(t)\}.$$

That is, every representative of H_j in $P(t)$ is at least as good as every representative of H_i in $P(t)$. With these definitions, we present a partial characterization of the broadest class of genetic algorithms:

Theorem 2. In any genetic algorithm using a monotonic selection algorithm and a monotonic fitness function, for any pair of hyperplanes H_i, H_j in $P(t)$,

$$H_i \leq_{D,t} H_j \rightarrow tsr(H_i, t) \leq tsr(H_j, t).$$

Proof. Without loss of generality, assume that we are maximizing over f. Consider two hyperplanes H_i and H_j such that $H_i \leq_{D,t} H_j$. That is,

$$\max \{f(x) \mid x \in H_i \cap P(t)\} \leq \min \{f(x) \mid x \in H_j \cap P(t)\}.$$

Since the fitness function is monotonic,

$$\max \{u(x) \mid x \in H_i \cap P(t)\} \leq \min \{u(x) \mid x \in H_j \cap P(t)\}.$$

Since the selection algorithm is monotonic,

$$\max \{tsr(x) \mid x \in H_i \cap P(t)\} \leq \min \{tsr(x) \mid x \in H_j \cap P(t)\}.$$

The preceding line and (1) yield that $tsr(H_i,t) \leq tsr(H_j,t)$.
□

Comparing Theorem 1 and Theorem 2, we see that by substantially weakening the conclusion, we can include a much broader class of genetic algorithms in the characterization. There is certainly room for many theorems between Theorem 1 and Theorem 2 that describe the behavior of interesting classes of genetic algorithms. We strongly encourage others to help fill this gap. Still, Theorem 2 is more subtle than it may first appear. For one thing, it allows a characterization of the behavior of genetic algorithms in terms of the objective function: We say that hyperplane H_i is *completely dominated by* H_j ($H_i \leq_D H_j$) if

$$\max \{\alpha f(x) \mid x \in H_i\} \leq \min \{\alpha f(x) \mid x \in H_j\}. \quad (12)$$

That is, every possible representative of H_j is at least as good as every representative of H_i as every possible representative of H_i.

Corollary 2. In any genetic algorithm using a monotonic selection algorithm and a monotonic fitness function, for any pair of hyperplanes H_i, H_j,

$$H_i \leq_D H_j \rightarrow (\forall t)\, tsr(H_i,t) \leq tsr(H_j,t).$$

That is, if H_j completely dominates H_i, then H_j grows at least as fast as H_i in any generation in any genetic algorithm that satisfies the conditions of Theorem 2. Note that this statement is independent of the particular representatives of the two hyperplanes at time t.

Baker (1989) has called genetic algorithms that use a monotonic selection algorithm and a monotonic fitness function *reliably consistent (RC)* genetic algorithms. The following definitions motivate this terminology. We say that hyperplane H_i is *less reliable than* H_j in $P(t)$ if

$$\min \{\alpha f(x) \mid x \in H_i \cap P(t)\} \leq \min \{\alpha f(x) \mid x \in H_j \cap P(t)\}$$

and

$$\max \{\alpha f(x) \mid x \in H_j \cap P(t)\} \leq \max \{\alpha f(x) \mid x \in H_i \cap P(t)\}$$

and at least one of the inequalities is strict. By this definition, if H_i is less reliable than H_j then H_i has a larger range of fitness values than does H_j. Furthermore, H_j dominates any hyperplane that is dominated by H_i, and H_j is dominated by any hyperplane that dominates H_i. It follows that RC genetic algorithms have the property that, if hyperplane H_j is more reliable than H_i, then Theorem 2 specifies the growth rates of at least as many hyperplanes relative to H_j as it specifies relative to H_i. Admittedly, this is a rather weak description of the implicit parallelism in RC genetic algorithms, but we offer it as a small step in the direction of providing useful theoretic descriptions of the behavior of genetic algorithms.

6. EMPIRICAL CONSIDERATIONS

Baker (1989) describes extensive empirical comparisons of genetic algorithms that use a broad range of selection algorithms. These include:

- Proportional selection, described by (1);
- Linear rank selection, described by (3);
- Selection algorithms that enforce upper bounds on individual *tsr* values;
- Selection algorithms that enforce lower bounds on the *reproductive rate*, i.e., the percentage of individuals that have at least one offspring;
- Selection by deletion, in which part of the population is deleted and replaced by new individuals; and
- Hybrid algorithms that switch between two selection algorithms, e.g., proportional selection and ranking, based on measures that predict rapid convergence.

It is easy to show that a genetic algorithm that uses any one of these selection algorithms and a monotonic fitness function is in the class of RC genetic algorithms. Furthermore, Baker shows that for any such genetic algorithm, empirical tuning of the parameters defining the selection method yields an algorithm with high performance over an extensive test suite that includes:

- De Jong's classical test functions
- Functions designed to promote premature convergence
- Optimization problems derived from the image registration domain
- Traveling salesman problems.

These diverse genetic algorithms all satisfy Theorem 2 but only the proportional selection algorithm satisfied Theorem 1. Clearly, Theorem 2 does not provide sufficient conditions for good performance in a genetic algorithm, but neither does Theorem 1 provide necessary conditions. There is still much work to do to characterize the behavior of various classes of genetic algorithms.

Progress in this direction will require the development of new concepts that describe aspects of genetic algorithms. Baker's work suggests that the selection algorithm's *sensitivity* to the objective function may be a useful concept. Some selection algorithms are more sensitive than others, meaning that the growth rates of hyperplanes are more closely tied to the values of the objective function. At one extreme, proportional selection permits an individual's *tsr* to range anywhere from 0 to N, depending on the values of the objective function. Selection by linear ranking is less sensitive, since the maximum *tsr* for any individual is 2, regardless of the value of the objective function. And at the other extreme, one form of the deletion algorithm replaces individuals whose fitness falls below some threshold (e.g., $\bar{u}(t)/2$) with a new random individual. The remaining individuals are all assigned a *tsr* of 1, regardless of objective function value. Intuitively, sensitivity seems to be a desirable feature in that the objective function provides the primary knowledge about the payoff associated with areas of the search space. However, the performance of the genetic algorithm using selection by deletion compared well with other genetic algorithms, given the proper settings for parameters that control the deletion algorithm. So, sensitivity is not a necessary feature of successful genetic algorithms. In fact, sensitivity often conflicts with another goal of genetic algorithms -- maintaining sufficient diversity in the population to support continued search. For example, consider two objective functions $f_1(x) = x$ and $f_2(x) = x^{10}$. Highly sensitive selection algorithms tend to converge prematurely on steep functions such as f_2, whereas less sensitive algorithms can handle either function equally well. In fact, ranking performs identically on f_1 and f_2, evolving the same sequence of populations in either case.

These observations suggest that one way to fill the gap between Theorem 1 and Theorem 2 is to include conditions specifying the sensitivity of a selection algorithm. For example, by requiring strict inequalities in (9)-(12), we get the following results:

Theorem 3. In any genetic algorithm using a (strictly) monotonic selection algorithm and a (strictly) monotonic fitness function, for any pair of hyperplanes H_i, H_j in $P(t)$,

$$H_i <_{D,t} H_j \rightarrow tsr(H_i, t) < tsr(H_j, t).$$

Corollary 3. In any genetic algorithm using a (strictly) monotonic selection algorithm and a (strictly) monotonic fitness function, for any pair of hyperplanes H_i, H_j,

$$H_i <_D H_j \rightarrow (\forall t) \, tsr(H_i, t) < tsr(H_j, t).$$

That is, if H_j completely dominates H_i in the strict sense that every representative of H_j is strictly better than every representative of H_i, then H_j grows exponentially faster than H_i in any genetic algorithm that satisfies the conditions in Theorem 3.

This result is just one example of how we might describe the search behavior of an interesting class of genetic algorithms in terms of the objective function. Presumably, there are other theorems that characterize the behavior of good genetic algorithms that do not meet the requirements of strict monotonicity, such as the one based on deletion mentioned above. We leave such further developments to future research.

7. SUMMARY

One of the main points of this paper is that it is useful to separate the notion of *implicit parallelism* in genetic algorithms, i.e. the simultaneous allocation of search effort to many hyperplanes at once, from the discussion of precisely *how much* effort is allocated to various regions of the search space. Doing so allows us to describe the implicit parallelism shown by many varieties of genetic algorithms.

We have shown that the Schema Theorem, by describing the behavior of genetic algorithms in terms of the *fitness* function rather than the *objective* function, does not explicitly prescribe a unique allocation of trials to competing hyperplanes. Theorem 1 shows how to characterize the search behavior of a large class genetic algorithms in terms of the objective function, but still fails to cover many successful genetic algorithms. Theorem 2 offers a description of the behavior of what seems to be the broadest possible class of genetic algorithms, but fails to discriminate the features of successful genetic algorithms from those of obviously degenerate search procedures. Theorem 3 is an example of an interesting characterization of the behavior of a restricted class of genetic algorithms. The empirical studies show that further effort is necessary to characterize the behavior of "good" genetic algorithms by filling in the gaps between Theorems 1 and 2.

This work has some important implications for the existing theory of genetic algorithms. The "well known, but poorly understood" (Goldberg, 1989; p. 40) claim that genetic algorithms process approximately N^3 hyperplanes in a population of size N has been supported by arguments that simply count the number of competing hyperplanes in a random population (Fitzpatrick & Grefenstette, 1988; Goldberg, 1989). Since the counting arguments assume independence of the structures in the population, the N^3 result applies only to the first few generations of a genetic algorithm. But more importantly, our discussion of the k-armed bandits analogy shows that one cannot assume that the genetic algorithm treats every hyperplane competition as a k-armed bandit problem. Thus, more sophisticated methods are needed to quantify the parallelism of genetic algorithms.

Finally, this work suggests that a new approach is needed to characterize problems that may be difficult for genetic algorithms. Both Bethke (1981) and Goldberg (1987) assume that genetic algorithms proceed by solving k-armed bandit problems defined by competing short definition length hyperplanes, and therefore, problems in which such hyperplanes are "misleading" -- meaning that the hyperplanes with the best average payoff do not contain the true optimum -- are hard for genetic algorithms. Our discussion calls this assumption into question. Genetic algorithms do not in general proceed by estimating the average payoffs of short definition length hyperplanes. This faulty assumption may explain Goldberg's empirical findings that genetic algorithms usually converge to the correct solution even for his "deceptive" problems unless severely hampered by bias in the initial population (Goldberg, 1987).

ACKNOWLEDGEMENTS

Thanks to Ken De Jong, Helen Cobb, Connie Ramsey, and Bill Spears, whose comments greatly improved the final version of this paper.

REFERENCES

Baker, J. E. (1985). Adaptive selection methods for genetic algorithms. *Proceedings of the International Conference Genetic Algorithms and Their Applications* (pp. 101-111). Pittsburgh, PA.

Baker, J. E. (1987). Reducing bias and inefficiency in the selection algorithm. *Proceedings of the Second International Conference Genetic Algorithms and Their Applications* (pp. 14-21). Cambridge, MA: Erlbaum.

Baker, J. E. (1989). *Analysis of the effects of selection in genetic algorithms*, Doctoral dissertation, Department of Computer Science, Vanderbilt University, Nashville.

Bethke, A. D. (1981). *Genetic algorithms as function optimizers*, Doctoral dissertation, Department Computer and Communication Sciences, University of Michigan, Ann Arbor.

Bridges C. L. and D. E. Goldberg, (1987). An analysis of reproduction and crossover in a binary-encoded genetic algorithm. *Proceedings of the Second International Conference Genetic Algorithms and Their Applications* (pp. 9-13). Cambridge, MA: Erlbaum.

De Jong, K. A. (1975). *Analysis of the behavior of a class of genetic adaptive systems*, Doctoral dissertation, Department Computer and Communication Sciences, University of Michigan, Ann Arbor.

Fitzpatrick, J. M. and J. J. Grefenstette (1983). Personal communication.

Fitzpatrick, J. M. and J. J. Grefenstette (1988) Genetic algorithms in noisy environments. *Machine Learning, 3(2/3)*, (pp. 101-120).

Gillies, A. M. (1985). *Machine learning procedures for generating image domain feature detectors*. Doctoral dissertation, Department Electrical Engineering and Computer Science, University of Michigan, Ann Arbor.

Goldberg, D. E. (1987). Simple genetic algorithms and the minimal, deceptive problem. In *Genetic algorithms and simulated annealing*. D. Davis (ed.), London: Pitman Press.

Goldberg, D. E. (1989). *Genetic algorithms in search, optimization, and machine learning*. Reading: Addison-Wesley.

Grefenstette, J. J. (1986). Optimization of control parameters for genetic algorithms. *IEEE Trans. Systems, Man, and Cybernetics, SMC-16(1)*, (pp. 122-128).

Holland, J. H. (1975). *Adaptation in natural and artificial systems*. Ann Arbor: University Michigan Press.

Whitley, D. (1987). Using reproductive evaluation to improve genetic search and heuristic discovery. *Proceedings of the Second International Conference Genetic Algorithms and Their Applications* (pp. 108-115). Cambridge, MA: Erlbaum.

Sizing Populations for Serial and Parallel Genetic Algorithms

David E. Goldberg
Department of Engineering Mechanics
The University of Alabama
Tuscaloosa, AL 35487

Reproduced with permission from *The Proceedings of the Third International Conference on Genetic Algorithms*, Morgan Kaufmann Publishers, San Mateo, California, 1989. Not for further reproduction or distribution without written consent of the publisher and author.

Abstract

Choosing a suitable population size is a key decision faced by all users of genetic algorithms and genetics-based machine learning systems. This paper extends the existing theory of optimal initial population size to include computations performed on either serial or parallel processors. Exact and asymptotic formulas are presented for the expected number of schemata in a population of strings. These calculations are used to derive a rational figure of merit for population size determination: the approximate rate of schema processing. Golden search is then used to calculate population size values that maximize this criterion over a range of string length values and for machines with varying degrees of parallelism.

1 Introduction

Choosing the population size for a genetic algorithm (GA) is a fundamental decision faced by all GA users. On the one hand, if too small a population size is selected, the genetic algorithm will converge too quickly, with insufficient processing of too few schemata. On the other hand, a population with too many members results in long waiting times for significant improvement, especially when evaluation of individuals within a population must be performed wholly or partially in serial: the population is too large to get enough mixing of building blocks per unit of computation time. In a previous note (Goldberg, 1985), I investigated some of the issues surrounding the processing of schemata in serial genetic algorithms. In this paper, I extend that work to include processing by computers operating at differing degrees of parallelism.

In the remainder of this paper, previous theoretical work related to population size is reviewed, and an extended calculation of expected numbers of schemata in populations of various sizes, alphabet cardinalities, string lengths, and required schema count values is de-veloped. Thereafter, the schema calculation is used to formulate a rough figure of merit for population size optimization—the approximate real-time rate of schema processing—and this figure of merit is maximized via golden search. The results from this calculation and existing empirical studies of population size are then compared qualitatively; a number of suggestions are made for applying and extending the theory.

2 Existing Theory of Population Size

Holland's $O(n^3)$ estimate of effective schema processing is the most frequently cited theoretical development related to population size. Simply stated, this computation says that the number of schemata processed effectively (those processed with an error rate less than a specified value) is proportional to the cube of the population size—is $O(n^3)$. Unfortunately, many have taken this calculation out of Holland's original context and used it to justify the selection of ever larger population sizes. In a previous note (Goldberg, 1985), I rederived Holland's bound to show its underlying assumptions and to demonstrate the fallacy of such reasoning.

In that same note, I also calculated the expected number of unique schemata in a population of strings of specified length. I then used that calculation to define a figure of merit—the excess number of schemata per population member—and subsequently optimized that figure of merit over a range of string lengths. When properly applied, this theory seems to work well. One study (Pettey et al., 1987) reports good results in sizing hypercube subpopulations using this theory. Unfortunately, this theory, like Holland's before it, has been taken out of context. Robertson (1988) applied the theory without correction to some classifier system results obtained on a massively parallel computer and found that the theory underpredicted the population size one should take. Because the original theory was derived for serial genetic algorithms (the only kind prevalent in 1985), Robertson's results are hardly surprising. Nonetheless, Robertson's work indirectly raises the right question. How might this theory be extended to calculate population sizes for genetic algorithms running at varying degrees of parallelism? In what follows, we examine the computations necessary to answer exactly this question.

3 Computing the Expected Number of Schemata

To develop a rational figure of merit for population size optimization, we first need to know the expected number of schemata contained in a randomly chosen population of given size. This calculation was performed in the previous note (Goldberg, 1985). We repeat the calculation here to better understand its assumptions. We also extend the calculation to cases where more than a single copy of each schema is required and to cases with other than binary alphabets.

3.1 The Basic Schema Function $\mathcal{S}$

To count the expected number of unique schemata in a population, consider the probability of having a particular schema of order i in a population of size n when the bit positions are equally likely ($p_1 = p_0 = \frac{1}{2}$). The probability of a single match may be calculated as

$$P(\text{single match of a schema of order } i) = \left(\frac{1}{2}\right)^i, \quad (1)$$

where i is the order (the number of fixed positions) in the schema. The chance of having no matches of a single order i schema in a population of size n may be calculated as

$$P(\text{no matches of an order } i \text{ schema}) = \left[1 - \left(\frac{1}{2}\right)^i\right]^n \quad (2)$$

or simply the product of the n failure probabilities. The probability of one or more successes may then be calculated as the complementary probability:

$$P(\text{at least one success}) = 1 - \left[1 - \left(\frac{1}{2}\right)^i\right]^n. \quad (3)$$

Over i fixed positions there are 2^i such schemata and over a string of length l there are $\binom{l}{i}$ sets of fixed positions. Thus, the expected number of schemata in a population of size n over strings of length l may be calculated as the following sum:

$$\mathcal{S}(n,l) = \sum_{i=0}^{l} \binom{l}{i} 2^i \left\{ 1 - \left[1 - \left(\frac{1}{2}\right)^i\right]^n \right\}. \quad (4)$$

We call this function the *schema function*, and its value is graphed versus population size at different string lengths in Figure 1. At a population size $n = 1$ the schema function always has a value of 2^l because a single string is itself a representative of 2^l different schemata (we can have a fixed bit or a * at all l positions). As the population size becomes very large, the number of schemata approaches 3^l, the maximum possible for binary strings of length l. Additional information about the behavior of the number of schemata in a randomly generated population may be gained by considering asymptotes at both high and low values of population size.

3.2 Asymptotes and Such

Equation 4 may be simplified immediately with a single application of the binomial theorem:

$$\mathcal{S}(n,l) = 3^l - \sum_{i=0}^{l} \binom{l}{i} 2^i \left[1 - \left(\frac{1}{2}\right)^i\right]^n. \quad (5)$$

At large values of population size, the term

$$\left[1 - \left(\frac{1}{2}\right)^i\right]^n$$

is well approximated by the expression $e^{-n/2^i}$. Considering only the last term, we obtain the asymptotic expansion for the schema function as follows:

$$\mathcal{S}(n,l) \approx 3^l - 2^l e^{-n/2^l}. \quad (6)$$

Additional terms may be added to the expansion to provide greater accuracy in the approximation at lower population sizes (those lower than $n \approx 2^l$), but even this level of approximation is useful to explain the behavior of the schema function at high n values. Defining $\hat{\mathcal{S}} = 3^l - 0.9 \cdot 2^l$ (the number of schemata within 9/10 of a string population of the maximum number of schemata) and defining $\hat{n}$ as the population size where this number of schemata occurs (where $0.9 = e^{-n/2^l}$), an expression relating $\hat{\mathcal{S}}$ and $\hat{n}$ may be obtained. This relationship overlays the curves of Figure 1 as a dashed line, separating the behavior of the schema function at medium and high population sizes.

The behavior of the schema function may also be approximated at small population sizes. To do this, consider Equation 5 and expand the term $\left[1 - \left(\frac{1}{2}\right)^i\right]^n$ using the binomial theorem:

$$\mathcal{S}(n,l) = 3^l - \sum_{i=0}^{l} \binom{l}{i} 2^i \sum_{j=0}^{n} \binom{n}{j} (-1)^j \left(\frac{1}{2}\right)^{ij}. \quad (7)$$

Reversing the order of summation and again applying the binomial theorem, we may place the schema function in n-form (as opposed to the previous l-form):

$$\mathcal{S}(n,l) = 3^l - \sum_{j=0}^{n} \binom{n}{j} (-1)^j \left[1 + \left(\frac{1}{2}\right)^{j-1}\right]^l. \quad (8)$$

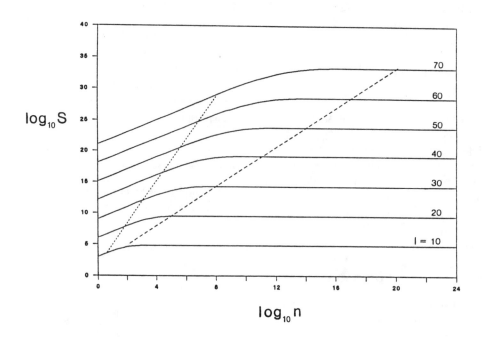

Figure 1: The expected number of schemata $\mathcal{S}$ plotted as a function, of population size n at different string lengths l. Upper and lower bounds on approximate function values are shown by dashed lines

At low values of population size, the schema function may be well approximated by the first two terms of this series:

$$\mathcal{S}(n,l) \approx 3^l - 3^l + n2^l = n2^l. \tag{9}$$

This corresponds to the well-known bound on the number of schemata contained in a population of given size and length (Goldberg, 1989a; Holland, 1975). If we consider the next term in the series, a simple expression may be developed for the dividing line between low-n and intermediate-n behavior. Defining $\check{\mathcal{S}}$ as the number of schemata where the linear model $n2^l$ diverges from the actual model by approximately 10 percent, and defining $\check{n}$ as the population size where that divergence occurs, we may obtain the following relationships defining the dividing line:

$$\check{n} = 0.2 \left(\frac{4}{3}\right)^l, \tag{10}$$

$$\check{\mathcal{S}} = \check{n}2^l. \tag{11}$$

Better approximations to low-n behavior may be obtained by considering more terms in the n-form series.

3.3 Extensions of the Basic Formula

The schema function may be extended to consider a higher degree of required duplication and to permit calculations for strings over alphabets with cardinality greater than two.

Counting schemata only when they are represented by two, three, or more copies makes sense if we acknowl-

edge the noisy sampling process inherent in genetic algorithms; one copy may not be enough to insure the life of potentially useful schemata.

To count the expected number of schemata with a required degree of duplication, we define the parameter c to be the number of copies required. Thereafter, we take the previous computation and subtract off the binomially distributed probability of n failures, $n-1$ failures, and so on for a total of c terms in the inner summation:

$$\mathcal{S}(n,l,c) = 3^l -$$
$$\sum_{i=0}^{l} \binom{l}{i} 2^i \sum_{j=n-c+1}^{n} \binom{n}{j} \left[1 - \left(\tfrac{1}{2}\right)^i\right]^j \left(\tfrac{1}{2}\right)^{i(n-j)}. \tag{12}$$

The inner sum may be approximated by a Poisson distribution to yield a simplified expression describing behavior at large population size values.

The schema function may also be extended to count expected numbers of schemata in strings over alphabets of cardinality greater than two. Assuming that initial populations are chosen randomly with equal probabilities for all k members of the permissible alphabet, the arguments of the previous sections may be extended to the k-alphabet immediately:

$$\mathcal{S}(n,l,c,k) = (k+1)^l -$$
$$\sum_{i=0}^{l} \binom{l}{i} k^i \sum_{j=n-c+1}^{n} \binom{n}{j} \left[1 - \left(\tfrac{1}{k}\right)^i\right]^j \left(\tfrac{1}{k}\right)^{i(n-j)}. \tag{13}$$

This form of the equation may be used to analyze the

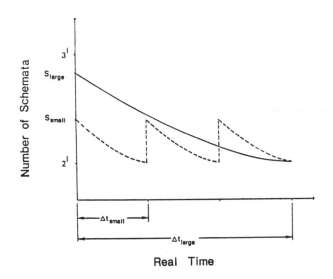

Figure 2: Comparison of large and small populations. The small population may be run to convergence and be restarted several times before the large population converges.

schema content of classifier system populations or non-binary genetic algorithms. In the remainder of the paper, we will consider the simpler two-parameter schema function of Equation 5.

4 Population Size Optimization

The calculations of the previous sections are useful in that they allow us to calculate with accuracy the expected number of schemata contained in randomly generated populations. More than this, they permit the development of a rational objective function for sizing GA populations. To do this, we must consider the rate of schema processing as genetic algorithms converge.

4.1 The Rate of Schema Processing

Although there are many ways to devise a figure of merit related to optimum population size, a rational approach must incorporate at least two things: the numbers of schemata processed and the time of their processing. To see this more clearly, consider the schematic representation of convergence in two different GAs (Figure 2), one with a large population and one with a small population. Initially starting from a randomly generated population, higher numbers of schemata are contained in the larger population (as we should expect from our calculations of the previous section). As the GAs run, it is difficult to predict exactly the number of schemata contained in each GA, but one thing is certain. Given enough time, the pressure applied through step after repeated step of reproduction will cause both GAs to converge. This is illustrated in the figure, where the schema content of both

the large and small populations is shown to approach 2^l schemata asymptotically.

Although similar in their asymptotes, the large and small population GAs differ in the time required to effectively reach the asymptote. This difference in real-time convergence can come from two factors. Small populations converge in fewer generations than do large populations, and small populations take less time to evaluate a given generation than do large populations (unless the computations are perfectly parallel). This faster convergence in real time provides the opportunity to restart the small-population GA a number of times while the large-population GA is still converging. Although some GA users steadfastly refuse to take this opportunity near convergence (thereby permitting the GA to degenerate to random search about the current solution or solutions), if one is interested in optimizing off-line performance (convergence to the near best), this opportunity should not be passed up; it is also an opportunity that cannot be ignored in devising a rational figure of merit for population size optimization.

This reasoning immediately suggests one figure of merit that might be used to try to optimize GA performance: the average real-time rate of schema processing $\frac{dS}{dt}$. If we can keep the rate of schema mixing high under the pressure of reproduction, crossover, and other genetic operators, it seems reasonable to suggest that we will get better answers than if we allow the schema turnover to languish.

Although detailed evaluation of this particular figure of merit requires knowledge of the shape of the schemata versus time curve, we can easily approximate the schema processing rate with a finite difference:

$$\frac{dS}{dt} \approx \frac{\Delta S}{\Delta t} = \frac{S_0 - 2^l}{\Delta t}, \qquad (14)$$

where S_0 is the initial number of schemata contained in the population, 2^l is the final number of schemata contained in the population, and Δt is the elapsed real time to convergence.

The development of the schema function S allows us to calculate the numerator of this expression. To calculate the denominator, as was hinted earlier, we need to consider two factors: the number of generations to convergence (n_c) and the computation time per generation (t_c). Thus the overall elapsed time may be calculated as follows:

$$\Delta t = n_c t_c. \qquad (15)$$

These computations are performed in the next two sections.

4.2 Estimating the Number of Generations to Convergence

To calculate the number of generations to convergence in a population of structures, consider the simplest possible situation, where only two possible structures exist: 1 and 0. Assume further that there is a proportion of 1 structures at time t equal to $P_1(t)$, and suppose that structures 0 and 1 have deterministic fitness values f_0 and f_1. By the schema theorem (Goldberg, 1989), we may calculate the proportion of 1 structures in the next generation as follows:

$$P_1(t+1) = \frac{f_1 P_1(t)}{f_1 P_1(t) + [1 - P_1(t)] f_0}. \quad (16)$$

Dropping the subscript 1, letting r equal the fitness ratio f_1/f_0, and taking the equation to the limit, we obtain a differential equation for the better structure proportion:

$$\frac{dP}{dt} = \frac{(r-1)[P(1-P)]}{(r-1)P + 1}. \quad (17)$$

Integrating by elementary means we obtain the solution

$$U = U_i e^{(r-1)t}, \quad (18)$$

where the auxiliary variable U is defined as

$$U = \frac{P}{(1-P)^r}, \quad (19)$$

and the subscript i denotes the initial time ($t = 0$).

This equation is useful in its own right, but here we are interested in calculating the number of generations to convergence n_c. Suppose a run is started with an initial proportion of individuals P_i, and further suppose that the population is permitted to converge to a final proportion P_f. Substituting these values into Equations 18 and 19, we obtain the following result:

$$(r-1)n_c = \ln\left[\frac{P_f}{(1-P_f)^r} \frac{(1-P_i)^r}{P_i}\right], \quad (20)$$

where we recognize that the time variable in the previous solution is in generational time units. Assuming that the better solution exists initially at a proportion $P_i = \gamma$ and assuming we let the run proceed until a final proportion $P_f = (1 - \gamma)$, we obtain the following result:

$$n_c = \frac{r+1}{r-1} \ln\left(\frac{1-\gamma}{\gamma}\right). \quad (21)$$

If the proportion γ is assumed to be a constant independent of population size, this computation tells us that the number of generations to convergence is of order $O(1)$: the number of generations to convergence is constant regardless of population size. If the population is permitted to converge to the bitter end, we can assume that we start with one better individual and end with all but one of the slots in the population filled by better individuals. We may then calculate n_c by making the substitution $\gamma = 1/n$ as follows:

$$n_c = \frac{r+1}{r-1} \ln(n-1). \quad (22)$$

Ignoring the r-related coefficient and recognizing that $\ln(n-1)$ and $\ln n$ are indistinguishable at large n values, we obtain the result that the number of generations n_c is of order $O(\ln n)$. Thus, depending on how far one lets the GA go, the number of generations to convergence is either a constant or a logarithmic function of the population size.

Of course, this computation is only half of our Δt story. In the next section, we calculate the functional form of the computation time per generation t_c.

4.3 Serial Meets Parallel: Computation Time per Generation

To round out the previously proposed figure of merit, we need to estimate the functional form of the computational time per generation. This requires that we evaluate the tasks being performed in a generation and consider those in the context of the degree of parallelism available in the computer system we are using.

During a generation of a genetic algorithm two major tasks are performed:

- genetic operators;

- function evaluations.

We ignore minor differences between parallel and serial implementations of the genetic operators and consider that the amount of computation required during a generation goes up in proportion to n. On a serial machine, this computation must be taken one step at a time and the computation time per generation is simply $t_c = O(n)$. On a perfectly parallel machine with n processors the work may be equally divided among the different processors without overhead and the computation time is $t_c = O(1)$—the computations can be performed in constant time.

Non-ideal parallel computers decrease in efficiency as the number of processors increases. Defining ρ as the ratio of parallel to serial machine speed and permitting a power law relationship of the form $\rho = n^\beta$, where β is the degree of parallelization, we may calculate the computation per time step t_c quite directly:

$$t_c = n^{1-\beta}. \quad (23)$$

Comparing this relationship to the discussion of the previous paragraph, we recognize that $\beta = 0$ corresponds to a serial machine and $\beta = 1$ corresponds to a perfectly parallel machine.

4.4 A Figure of Merit: Approximate Average Rate of Schema Processing

We may now combine the results of our tortuous journey to devise a reasonable figure of merit for population size optimization. Taking the initial value of the number of

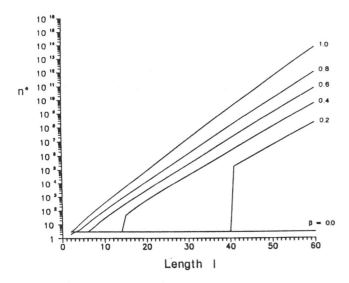

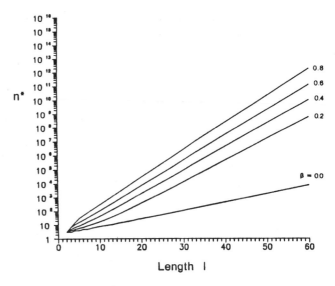

Figure 3: Optimal population size n^* as a function of string length at various values of parallelization parameter β with the number of generations to convergence a logarithmic function of n ($n_c = O(\ln n)$)

Figure 4: Optimal population size n^* as a function of string length at various values of parallelization parameter β with the number of generations to convergence a constant ($n_c = O(1)$)

schemata contained within a population minus the number of schemata left in the population at convergence, dividing by the estimate of the time to convergence, and dropping any superfluous constants of proportionality, we obtain the following figure of merit $\mathcal{M}$ related to effective schema processing:

$$
\begin{aligned}
\mathcal{M}(n, l, \beta) &= \frac{\Delta \mathcal{S}}{\Delta t}, \\
&= \frac{\mathcal{S}_0 - 2^l}{n_c t_c}, \\
&= \frac{\mathcal{S}(n, l) - 2^l}{n_c n^{1-\beta}}.
\end{aligned} \tag{24}
$$

Actually, this equation represents two figures of merit, depending on the convergence conditions we assume. Referring back to the previous discussion of the number of generations to convergence, recall that we can obtain constant time or logarithmic time estimates depending upon the degree of convergence we assume. A computer program has been developed to maximize the figure of merit under either assumption for any l or β values.

4.5 Golden Search Finds Optimal Population Size Values

Results from this program are displayed in Figures 3 (logarithmic n_c) and 4 (constant n_c) and tabulated in Table 1.

It is of particular interest to examine the results at the two ends of the serial-parallel machine spectrum. For a serial machine ($\beta = 0$) we obtain a range of comparatively small population sizes for fixed l. At the low end

of the range, the assumption of logarithmic convergence time (Figure 3) yields a fixed value of $n^* = 3$ regardless of string length l. At first this might seem surprising; however, further reflection tells us that the number of schemata grows less quickly than $n2^l$. This fact, combined with a denominator proportional to $n \ln n$, immediately dictates the selection of the smallest population size possible ($n^* = 3$) for all string length values.[1]

Under the assumption of constant convergence time (Figure 4), serial GA population sizes remain relatively small, but increase exponentially with increasing string length. These results are identical to those presented in the earlier note (Goldberg, 1985). Although the previous work was motivated somewhat differently (back then I talked of excess schemata per population member), we can see now that those results were equivalent to maximizing the rate of schema processing under the assumption of a constant time to convergence.

For a perfectly parallel machine ($\beta = 1$), the assumption of logarithmic convergence time yields relatively large population sizes for optimal performance (Figure 3). The assumption of constant convergence time on

---

[1]The value $n^* = 3$ has been chosen because in an independent genetic algorithm three is the smallest population size that makes sense in connection with reproduction and crossover. This is so because in a population of size two or smaller we cannot select against a population member and still have a meaningful exchange of building blocks through recombination. Of course, if GAs can communicate, then selection against bad individuals can occur through interprocess exchange, but such action would violate the assumption of an independent GA.

Table 1: Optimal Population Size vs. β, l, and Convergence Assumption

l	$\beta = 1$	$\beta = .8$	$\beta = .6$	$\beta = .4$	$\beta = .2$	$\beta = 0$
			Logarithmic			
10	369	106	29	3	3	3
20	88095	13976	3288	599	3	3
30	1.74075E07	1.48220E06	2.58577E05	41159	3	3
40	3.14680E09	1.45522E08	1.86998E07	2.33867E06	3	3
50	5.38120E11	1.37269E10	1.30741E09	1.26195E08	6.16887E06	3
60	8.83975E13	1.26258E12	8.97892E10	6.66816E09	2.62081E08	3
			Constant			
10	∞	308	113	45	18	8
20	∞	30154	7389	1959	405	29
30	∞	2.86014E06	4.96557E05	95622	13735	116
40	∞	2.63783E08	3.32283E07	4.74523E06	4.91584E05	473
50	∞	2.38665E10	2.21466E09	2.37359E08	1.79852E07	1952
60	∞	2.12988E12	1.47152E11	1.19355E10	6.67984E08	8119

a perfectly parallel machine (not graphed) immediately suggests that optimal population sizes should be infinite. Although very large to infinite gives us a good bit of latitude in selecting population size, the basic message for highly parallel implementations of genetic algorithms is clear: choose as large a population size as you can.

4.6 Do Empirical Results Agree with the Theory?

Too few empirical studies have been performed to know whether the theory provides quantitatively accurate predictions; however, qualitatively, the theory seems to agree with current results.

Most studies of genetic algorithms before 1985 concerned only those programmed on serial machines. De Jong's dissertation (1975) suggested relatively small population sizes based on limited parametric studies on a five-problem suite. Grefenstette (1986) studied the optimization of genetic algorithm parameters using De Jong's problem suite and found that even smaller population sizes could be taken if a more accurate selection scheme was adopted.

More recently, several investigators have turned to implementations of genetic algorithms on parallel hardware. Pettey (Pettey et al., 1987) used my earlier results (Goldberg, 1985) to size subpopulation sizes on a hypercube with some success (each node on a hypercube is a relatively independent serial machine, so the success of the early serial results is not surprising). Robertson (1988) programmed a classifier system on a Connection Machine and obtained marginally better results with increasing n using population sizes up to $n = 8000$.

The limited numbers of empirical studies make it difficult to draw firm conclusions. Both theory and practice suggest relatively small population sizes on serial machines and relatively large to infinite population size on

parallel machines, but additional empirical investigation is required to consolidate these findings.

5 Applying and Extending the Theory

In this section, we examine some ways to apply and extend the theory of the previous sections, but before we do, we need to recap the underlying assumptions of the theory to prevent application of the theory to inappropriate situations.

The calculations of the previous section are predicated upon four assumptions:

- Maximum real-time rate of schema mixing yields maximum performance.

- Only one copy of a schema is required before counting it.

- All schemata are equally important to function optimization.

- Binary, fixed-length structures are processed.

All of the assumptions are open to question, and whether the theory is valid in a particular problem will depend on how well the assumptions are met.

The primary assumption of this study, that maximum schema turnover yields best performance, seems reasonable and is supported by empirical studies, but we must remember that it is an assumption. To design a better figure of merit for a particular problem may require that we specify some information about the problem: order of deception (Goldberg, 1987, 1988a, 1989ab), signal-to-noise ratio, or other information.

The calculations of Section 4 assume that one copy of a schema is sufficient representation to count its presence. This is a computationally convenient place to start, but recalling the schema theorem, we know that the implicit parallelism works best when we have a reasonably accurate sample of important building blocks required to solve a particular problem; multiple copies may be required to accomplish this.

The calculations of Sections 3 and 4 both assume that all schemata are equally important. It is easy to design problems where this is not the case. For example, we may design functions where all schemata below a certain order are misleading (Bethke, 1980; Goldberg, 1988a, 1989b). In problems such as this it makes no sense to weight schemata of *lower* order in the figure of merit, because they cannot contribute to the construction of the necessary higher order building blocks.

The calculations of Section 4 assume that binary, fixed length structures are being processed. If this is not the case, the user should return to the results of Section 3 and generate tables and graphs for the alphabet being used.

With these assumptions in mind, the careful user should have little problem applying the results of this paper to his or her work. In the remainder of this section, we interpret the theory in the light of current population sizing practice. We also suggest ways to extend the theory to situations not covered by the assumptions of the particular calculations.

5.1 Serial Selection: Are We Doing It Well?

The theory immediately raises the question whether current standard practice makes good use of schemata on serial machines. Currently, populations ranging in size from 30 to 200 are typically chosen and run for some fixed number of function evaluations. The results of this paper suggest that smaller populations may be better and that a more appropriate stopping criterion would be based on the degree of convergence in population (the equations of Section 3 might provide useful prior estimates).

As an extreme case, recall that the logarithmic generations-to-convergence estimate yields an optimal population size of $n^* = 3$ regardless of the string length l. This result is somewhat startling. Although Grefenstette's recent results (1986) point to the use of smaller population sizes, nothing this small has ever been suggested (or tried). Of course, simply taking small population sizes and running them to convergence and letting them wiggle around due to mutation is not going to be very useful. On the other hand, if we restart populations when they converge (as was suggested in Figure 2), we may be able to keep the rate of useful schema processing high.[2]

More specifically, these results suggest that serial GAs should use a scheme along the following lines:

1. Randomly generate a small population.

2. Perform genetic operations until nominal convergence (as measured by bitwise convergence or some other reasonable measure).

3. Generate a new population by transferring the best individuals of the converged population to the new population and then generating the remaining individuals randomly.

4. Go to step 2 and repeat.

This procedure becomes intuitively more palatable, if we contrast how diversity is introduced into serial and parallel cases. In the ideal parallel case (using an assumption of constant convergence time), the theory suggests an infinite population size to obtain maximum mixing. This solution (even though it is unrealizable) introduces one large batch of diversity into a simulation at the beginning. Contrast this with the serial case where we are now suggesting that small batches of diverse points be injected into the population at regular intervals. If we don't take steps to reintroduce diversity, the ideal parallel case has an unfair raw material advantage (a diversity advantage) over the serial case. The theory suggests how to eliminate that advantage and maintain a high rate of schema processing.[3]

5.2 Perfectly Parallel: The More the Merrier

Application of the theory to parallel GAs is straightforward: if you have multiple processors, use them to sample more points per generation and you will be rewarded with a higher rate of schema processing. As new parallel hardware becomes more widely available, this will be easier to do. By using parallel processors, in a sense, we will be able to have our cake and eat it too. Not only will we be able to sample at high schema rates, we will also have the reliable schema averages that can be obtained only with large population sizes.

---

[2]Some caution should be exercised in taking the $n^* = 3$ result too literally, however. Recalling the assumptions of the calculation, we recognize that one copy of a schema may be insufficient to get a good average. Also, in problems with a high degree of deception, it is inappropriate to include the low-order schemata in the figure of merit. Nonetheless, these results suggest that small populations may be appropriate on serial machines if we are careful to restart the GA each time it converges.

[3]Since publishing this paper as a TCGA note in August, 1988, a number of people have checked this conjecture in various problems. Krishnakumar (1989) has obtained some supporting results on standard test functions and on a wind-shear controller tuning task. The latter application is particularly interesting because a light-footed, small-population GA is able to track a non-stationary wind-shear environment.

5.3 Multimodal Functions and Genetics-Based Machine Learning Systems

The results of this paper are strictly applicable to problems with a single answer. After all, we assumed that the end point of the converged solution was a single string (itself containing 2^l schemata). Many function optimization problems and all machine learning problems require that we search for a number of different solutions (rules). Fortunately, we may think of each of these solutions separately and simply take the population size recommended by the unmodified theory and multiply it by the number of solutions or rules we expect in the final population.

5.4 Extensions to the Theory

The major assumptions enumerated earlier in this section suggest several extensions to the computations of this paper:

1. Consider alphabets of higher cardinality.

2. Require a specified number of copies of each schema.

3. Exclude low-order schemata for problems of known deception.

4. Consider other non-uniform schema weighting functions.

The first two items, considering higher cardinality alphabets and requiring a specified number of copies, may be considered quite directly. To perform similar computations for problems with non-binary alphabets, Equation 13 may be incorporated into the figure of merit and maximized using golden search by the methods of Section 4. That the theory can be extended to such problems should not be taken as an endorsement of the use of higher cardinality alphabets. When designing GAs, users should remember the *principle of minimal alphabets* (Goldberg, 1988b, 1989a) which suggests that the smallest, convenient alphabet be used.

Incorporating a requirement for a specified number of copies in the figure of merit is also a direct extension of the computations of this paper. Doing so may be useful because it should help guarantee a sufficiently accurate average for each schema before it is counted. Suitable assumptions may be made about the prior distribution of fitness values, and these may be used to calculate the minimum number of copies required to reduce the confidence interval of specified level to a suitable range of values.

In some problems, it may be desirable to exclude low-order schemata from the figure of merit. This is particularly the case where low-order schemata are misleading (Goldberg, 1987, 1988a, 1989b). In such problems, low-order schemata with above average fitness values combine to form suboptimal higher order schemata. In these cases, populations must be sized to have a sufficient number of copies of the higher order schemata, because they are unlikely to be generated through the normal course of reproduction and recombination. To perform these computations, the lower limit of summation should be changed to be the lowest order of schema above which there is little or no deception. Performing the calculations in this manner suggests the possibility of a more general non-uniform weighting procedure for schemata of different order values. A weighting function $w(i)$ may be defined as a function of the order i; it may then be incorporated in the figure of merit, where calculations may proceed as before.

6 Conclusions

This paper has placed the theory of population sizing for serial and parallel GAs on firmer footing through the introduction and maximization of a rational figure of merit, the real-time rate of schema processing. The theory has calculated the expected number of schemata in a population of specified size and has continued by calculating the relationship between population size and the elapsed time to convergence of the population. These quantities have been combined to form the figure of merit, and this criterion has been optimized using golden search.

These computations have suggested that relatively small populations are appropriate for serial implementations and large populations are appropriate for perfectly parallel GAs. Additionally, several specific recommendations have been made for applying and extending this theory to problems not covered by the simplifying assumptions of this study.

Acknowledgments

This material is based upon work supported by the National Science Foundation under Grant MSM-8451610. I am grateful for support provided by the Alabama Research Institute, Digital Equipment Corporation, the Rowland Institute for Science, and Texas Instruments Incorporated. I also acknowledge the workmanlike programming assistance provided by Brad Korb at The University of Alabama.

References

Bethke, A. D. (1980). Genetic algorithms as function optimizers (Doctoral dissertation, University of Michigan). *Dissertation Abstracts International, 41*(9), 3503B. (University Microfilms No. 8106101)

De Jong, K. A. (1975). An analysis of the behavior of a class of genetic adaptive systems. (Doctoral dissertation, University of Michigan). *Dissertation Abstracts International, 36*(10), 5140B. (University Microfilms No. 76-9381)

Goldberg, D. E. (1985). *Optimal initial population size for binary-coded genetic algorithms* (TCGA Report No. 85001). Tuscaloosa: University of Alabama, The Clearinghouse for Genetic Algorithms.

Goldberg, D. E. (1987). Simple genetic algorithms and the minimal deceptive problem. In L. Davis (Ed.), *Genetic algorithms and simulated annealing* (pp. 74-88). London: Pitman.

Goldberg, D. E. (1988a). *Genetic algorithms and Walsh functions: Part I, a gentle introduction* (TCGA Report No. 88006). Tuscaloosa: University of Alabama, The Clearinghouse for Genetic Algorithms.

Goldberg, D. E. (1988b). *Zen and the art of genetic algorithms* (TCGA Report No. 88003). Tuscaloosa, AL: University of Alabama, The Clearinghouse for Genetic Algorithms.

Goldberg, D. E. (1989a). *Genetic algorithms in search, optimization, and machine learning.* Reading, MA: Addison-Wesley.

Goldberg, D. E. (1989b). *Genetic algorithms and Walsh functions: Part II, deception and its analysis* (TCGA Report No. 89001). Tuscaloosa: University of Alabama, The Clearinghouse for Genetic Algorithms.

Grefenstette, J. J. (1986). Optimization of control parameters for genetic algorithms. *IEEE Transactions on Systems, Man, and Cybernetics, SMC-16*(1), 122-128.

Holland, J. H. (1975). *Adaptation in natural and artificial systems.* Ann Arbor, MI: University of Michigan Press.

Krishnakumar, K. S. (1989). *Micro genetic algorithms for stationary and nonstationary function optimization.* Manuscript submitted for publication.

Pettey, C. B., Leuze, M. R., & Grefenstette, J. J. (1987). A parallel genetic algorithm. *Genetic algorithms and their applications: Proceedings of the Second International Conference on Genetic Algorithms*, 155-161.

Robertson, G. G. (1988). Population size in classifier systems. *Proceedings of the Fifth International Conference on Machine Learning*, 142-152.

Learning with Genetic Algorithms:
An Overview

KENNETH DE JONG   (KDEJONG@GMU90X.GMU.EDU)
Computer Science Department, George Mason University, Fairfax, VA 22030, U.S.A.

(Received: January 15, 1988)

(Revised: May 20, 1988)

Keywords: Genetic algorithms, competition-based learning, learning task programs, classifier systems

Abstract.   Genetic algorithms represent a class of adaptive search techniques that have been intensively studied in recent years. Much of the interest in genetic algorithms is due to the fact that they provide a set of efficient domain-independent search heuristics which are a significant improvement over traditional "weak methods" without the need for incorporating highly domain-specific knowledge. There is now considerable evidence that genetic algorithms are useful for global function optimization and NP-hard problems. Recently, there has been a good deal of interest in using genetic algorithms for machine learning problems. This paper provides a brief overview of how one might use genetic algorithms as a key element in learning systems.

1. Introduction

The variety and complexity of learning systems makes it difficult to formulate a universally accepted definition of learning. However, a common denominator of most learning systems is their capability for making *structural changes* to themselves over time with the intent of improving performance on tasks defined by their environment, discovering and subsequently exploiting interesting concepts, or improving the consistency and generality of internal knowledge structures.

Given this perspective, one of the most important means for understanding the strengths and limitations of a particular learning system is a precise characterization of the structural changes that are permitted and how such changes are made. In classical terms, this corresponds to a clear understanding of the space of possible structural changes and the legal operators for selecting and making changes.

This perspective also lets one more precisely state the goal of the research in applying genetic algorithms to machine learning, namely, to understand when and how genetic algorithms can be used to explore spaces of legal structural changes in a goal-directed manner. This paper summarizes our current understanding of these issues.

2. Exploiting the power of genetic algorithms

Genetic algorithms (GAs) are a family of adaptive search procedures that have been described and extensively analyzed in the literature (De Jong, 1980; Grefenstette, 1986; Holland, 1975). GAs derive their name from the fact that they are loosely based on models of genetic change in a population of individuals. These models consist of three basic elements: (1) a Darwinian notion of "fitness," which governs the extent to which an individual can influence future generations; (2) a "mating operator," which produces offspring for the next generation; and (3) "genetic operators," which determine the genetic makeup of offspring from the genetic material of the parents.

A key point of these models is that adaptation proceeds, not by making incremental changes to a single structure (e.g., Winston, 1975; Fisher, 1987), but by maintaining a population (or database) of structures from which new structures are created using genetic operators such as crossover and mutation. Each structure in the population has an associated *fitness* (goal-oriented evaluation), and these scores are used in a *competition* to determine which structures are used to form new ones.

There is a large body of both theoretical and empirical evidence showing that, even for very large and complex search spaces, GAs can rapidly locate structures with high fitness ratings using a database of 50–100 structures. Figure 1 gives an abstract example of how the fitness of individuals in a population improves over time. Readers interested in a more detailed discussion of GAs should see Holland (1975), De Jong (1980), and Grefenstette (1986).

The purpose of this paper is to understand when and how GAs can lead to goal-directed structural changes in learning systems. We are now in a position to make some general observations, which we will explore in more detail in subsequent sections.

The key feature of GAs is their ability to exploit accumulating information about an initially unknown search space in order to bias subsequent search into useful subspaces. Clearly, if one has a strong domain theory to guide the process of structural change, one would be foolish not to use it. However, for many practical domains of application, it is very difficult to construct such theories. If the space of legal structural changes is not too large, one can usually develop an enumerative search strategy with appropriate heuristic cutoffs to keep the computation time under control. If the search space is large, however, a good deal of time and effort can be spent in developing domain-specific heuristics with sufficient cutoff power. It is precisely in these circumstances (large, complex, poorly understood search spaces) that one should consider exploiting the power of genetic algorithms.

At the same time, one must understand the price to be paid for searching poorly understood spaces. It typically requires 500–1000 samples before genetic algorithms have sufficient information to strongly bias subsequent samples into useful subspaces. This means that GAs will not be appropriate search procedures for learning domains in which the evaluation of 500–1000 alternative structural changes is infeasible. The variety of current activity in using GAs for machine learning suggests that many interesting learning problems

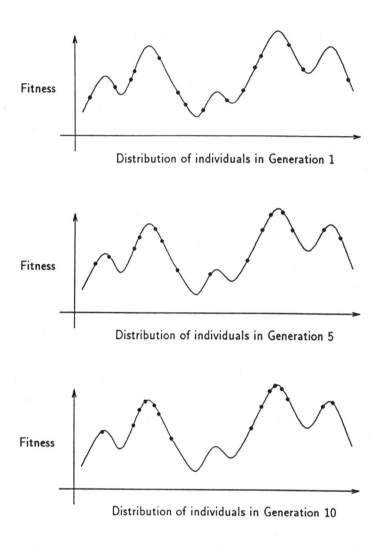

Figure 1. An abstract example of adaptive search using genetic algorithms.

fall into this category; i.e., involving large, complex, poorly understood search spaces in contexts that permit sampling rates sufficient to support GAs.

In discussing these activities, it will help to have a more concrete model of the architecture of a learning system that uses genetic algorithms. The simplest GA-based learning systems to describe are those whose goals are *performance oriented.* In this framework, the environment defines one or more tasks to be performed, and the learning problem involves both skill acquisition and skill refinement. It is generally useful to separate such systems (at least conceptually) into two subsystems as illustrated in Figure 2: a GA-based learning component charged with making appropriate structural changes, and a task component[1] whose performance-oriented behavior is to be improved.

---

[1]Within the machine learning literature, this is often called the *performance* component.

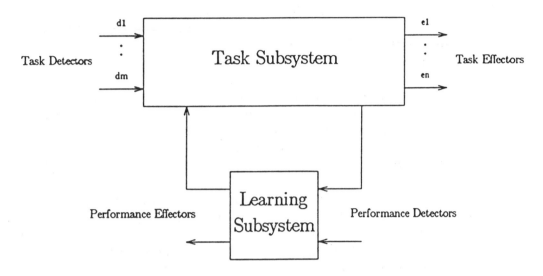

Figure 2. A performance-oriented learning system.

We are now in a position to describe how one might exploit the power of genetic algorithms in a learning system of the type depicted in Figure 2. The key idea is to define a space of *admissible* structures to be explored via GAs. Each point in this space represents the "genetic material" of a task subsystem in the sense that, when injected with this structure, its task performance is now well defined and can be measured. The learning strategy involves maintaining a population of tested structures and using GAs to generate new structures with better performance expectations.

In considering the kinds of structural changes that might be made to the task subsystem, there are a variety of approaches of increasing sophistication and complexity. The simplest and most straightforward approach is for the GAs to alter a set of parameters that control the behavior of a predeveloped, parameterized performance program. A second, more interesting, approach involves changing more complex data structures, such as "agendas," that control the behavior of the task subsystem. A third and even more intriguing approach involves changing the task program itself. The following sections explore each of these possibilities in more detail.

3. Using genetic algorithms to change parameters

A simple and intuitive approach to effecting behavioral changes in a performance system is to identify a key set of parameters that control the system's behavior and to develop a strategy for changing those parameters' values to improve performance. The primary advantage of this approach is that it immediately places us on the familiar terrain of parameter optimization problems, for which there is considerable understanding and guidance, and for which the simplest forms of GAs can be used. It is easy at first glance to discard this approach as trivial and not at all representative of what is meant by "learning." But note that significant behavioral changes can be achieved within this simple framework. Samuel's (1959, 1967) checker player is a striking example of the power of such an approach. If one views the adjustable weights and thresholds as parameters of a structurally-fixed neural network, then much of the research on neural net learning also falls into this category.

How can one use genetic algorithms to quickly and efficiently search for combinations of parameters that improve performance? The simplest and most intuitive approach views the parameters as genes and the genetic material of individuals as a fixed-length string of genes, one for each parameter. The crossover operator then generates new parameter combinations from existing good combinations in the current database (population) and mutation provides new parameter values.

There is considerable evidence, both experimental and theoretical, that GAs can home in on high-performance parameter combinations at a surprising rate (De Jong, 1975; Brindle, 1980; Grefenstette, 1986). Typically, even for large search spaces (e.g., 10^{30} points), acceptable combinations are found after only ten simulated generations. To be fair, however, there are several issues that can catch a GA practitioner off guard when attacking a particular problem in parameter modification.

The first issue involves the number of distinct values that genes (parameters) can take on. With population sizes generally in the 50–100 range, a given population can usually represent only a small fraction of the possible gene values. Since the only way of generating new gene values is via mutation, one can be faced with the following dilemma. If the mutation rate is too low, there can be insufficient global sampling to prevent premature convergence to local peaks. However, significantly increasing the rate of mutation can lead to a form of random search that decreases the probability that new individuals will have high performance. Fortunately, this problem has both a theoretical and a practical solution, although it is not obvious to the casual reader.

Holland (1975) provides an analysis of GAs which suggests that they are most effective when each gene takes on a small number of values, and that binary (two-valued) genes are in some sense optimal for GA-style adaptive search. This theoretical result translates rather naturally into what has now become standard practice in the GA community. Rather than representing a 20-parameter problem internally as strings of 20 genes (with each gene taking on many values), one uses a binary string representation that represents parameters as *groups* of binary-valued genes. Although the two spaces are equivalent in that both represent the same parameter space, GAs perform significantly better on the binary representation. This effect occurs because, in addition to mutation, crossover now generates new parameter values each time it combines part of a parameter's bits from one parent with those of another.

The simplest way to illustrate this point is to imagine the extreme case of a domain in which one must adjust a single parameter that can take on 2^{30} distinct values. Representing this problem internally as a one-gene problem renders crossover useless and leaves mutation as the only mechanism for generating new individuals. However, a 30-gene binary representation lets crossover play an active and crucial role in generating new parameter values with high performance expectations.

A second issue that arises in this context is that of convergence to a global optimum. Can we guarantee or expect with high probability that GAs will find the undisputed best combination of parameter settings for a particular problem? The answer is both "yes" and "no." Theoretically, every point in the search space has a nonzero probability of being sampled. However, for most problems of interest, the search space is so large that it is impractical to wait long enough for guaranteed global optimums. A better view is that GAs constitute powerful sampling heuristics that can rapidly find high-quality solutions in complex spaces.

In summary, one simple but effective approach is to restrict structural change to parameter modification and to use GAs to quickly locate useful combinations of parameter values. De Jong (1980) and Grefenstette (1986) provide more detailed examples of this approach.

4. Using genetic algorithms to change data structures

There are many problems for which the simple parameter modification approach is inappropriate, in the sense that more significant structural changes to task programs seem to be required. Frequently in these situations, a more complex data structure is intimately involved in controlling the behavior of the task, and so the most natural approach uses GAs to alter these key structures. For instance, such problems occur when the task system whose behavior is to be modified is designed with a top-level "agenda" control mechanism. Systems for traveling-salesman, bin-packing, and scheduling problems are frequently organized in this manner, as are systems driven by decision trees. In this context GAs must select data structures to be tested, evaluated, and subsequently used to fabricate better ones.

At first glance, this approach may not seem to introduce any difficulties for genetic algorithms, since it is usually not hard to "linearize" these data structures, map them into a string representation that a GA can manipulate, and then reverse the process to produce new data structures for evaluation. However, again there are some subtle issues, and the designer must be familiar with them in order to make effective use of GA-based learning systems.

As in the previous section on parameter spaces, these issues center around the way in which the space (in this case, a space of data structures) to be searched is represented internally for manipulation by GAs. One can easily invent internal string representations for agendas and other complex data structures, but for many of these schemes, almost every new structure produced by the standard crossover and mutation operators represents an *illegal* data structure!

An excellent example of this problem arises in using GAs to find good agendas (tours) for a traveling salesman who needs to visit N cities exactly once while minimizing the distance traveled. The most straightforward approach would internally represent a tour as N genes, with the value of each gene indicating the name of the next city to be visited. However, notice that GAs using the standard crossover and mutation operators will explore the space of all N-tuples of city names (most of which are illegal tours) when, in fact, it is the space of all *permutations* of the N city names that is of interest. The obvious problem is that, as N increases, the space of permutations becomes a vanishingly small subset of the space of N-tupples, and the powerful GA sampling heuristic has been rendered impotent by a poor choice of representation.

Fortunately, sensitivity to this issue is usually sufficient to avoid it in one of several ways. One approach is to design an alternative representation of the same space for which the traditional genetic operators are appropriate. GA researchers have taken this approach on a variety of such problems, including the traveling-salesman problem (e.g., see Grefenstette, Gopal, Rosmaita, & Van Gucht, 1985).

An equally useful alternative is to select different genetic operators that are more appropriate to "natural representations." For example, in the case of traveling salesman problems, a genetic-like inversion operator (which can be viewed as a particular kind of permutation operator) is clearly a more natural operator. Similarly, one can define representation-sensitive crossover and mutation operators to assure that offspring represent legal points in the solution space (e.g., see Goldberg & Lingle, 1985; Davis, 1985).

The key point here is that there is nothing sacred about the traditional string-oriented genetic operators. The mathematical analysis of GAs indicates that they work best when the internal representation encourages the emergence of useful building blocks that can subsequently be combined with each other to improve performance. String representations are just one of many ways of achieving this goal.

5. Using Genetic algorithms to change executable code

So far we have explored two approaches to using GAs to effect structural changes to task subsystems: (1) by changing critical parameter values, and (2) by changing key data structures. In this section we discuss a third possibility: effecting behavioral changes in a task subsystem by changing the task program itself. Although there is nothing fundamentally different between a task program that interprets an agenda data structure and one that executes a LISP program, generally the space of structural changes to executable code is considerably larger and very complex. In any case, there is a good deal of interest in systems that learn at this level, and the remainder of the paper will discuss how GAs can be used in such systems.

5.1 Choosing a programming language

Since our goal is to use genetic algorithms to evolve entire task programs, it is important to choose a task programming language that is well suited to manipulation by genetic operators. At first glance, this does not seem to be much of an issue, since programs written in conventional languages like FORTRAN and PASCAL (or even less conventional ones like LISP and PROLOG) can be viewed as linear strings of symbols. This is certainly the way they are treated by editors and compilers in current program development environments. However, it is also clear that this "natural" representation is disastrous for traditional GAs, since standard operators like crossover and mutation produce few syntactically correct programs and even fewer that are semantically correct.

One alternative is to devise new language-specific genetic operators that preserve at least the syntactic (and hopefully, the semantic) integrity of the programs being manipulated. Unfortunately, the syntactic and semantic complexity of traditional languages makes it difficult to develop such operators. An obvious next step would be to focus on less traditional languages with simpler syntax and semantics (e.g., "pure" LISP), thus having the potential for reasonable genetic operators with the required properties. There have been a number of activities in this area (e.g., see Fujiki & Dickinson, 1987).

However, pure LISP shares an important feature with more traditional languages: it is procedural in nature, and procedural representations have properties that cause difficulty for GA applications. One obvious problem involves order dependencies; interchanging two lines of code can render a program meaningless. Another is the occurrence of context-sensitive interpretations; minor changes to a section of code, such as the insertion or deletion of a punctuation symbol, can change the entire meaning of the succeeding code. De Jong (1985) presents a more detailed discussion of these representation problems.

These representational issues are not new. Holland (1975) anticipated them and proposed a family of languages (called *broadcast* languages) that were designed to overcome the problems described above. It is now clear that broadcast languages are a subset of a more general class of languages known as *production systems* (Newell, 1973; Neches, Langley, & Klahr, 1987). Production systems (PSs) continue to reassert their usefulness across a wide range of activities, from compiler design to expert systems; thus, a good deal of time and effort has gone into studying their use in evolving task programs with genetic algorithms.

5.2 Learning production-system programs

One reason that production systems have emerged as a favorite programming paradigm in both the expert system and machine learning communities is that they provide a representation of knowledge that can *simultaneously* support two kinds of activities: (1) treating knowledge as data to be manipulated as part of a knowledge-acquisition and refinement process, and (2) treating knowledge as an executable entity to be used in performing a particular task (Buchanan & Mitchell, 1978; Hedrick, 1976). This is particularly true of data-driven PSs such as OPS5 (Forgy, 1981), in which the production rules making up a program are treated as an unordered set of rules whose left-hand sides independently and in parallel monitor changes in the environment.

It should be obvious that this same programming paradigm offers significant advantages for GA applications. In fact, it has precisely the same characteristics as Holland's early broadcast languages. As a consequence, we will focus on PSs whose programs consist of unordered rules, and describe how GAs can be used to search the space of PS programs for useful rule sets.

To anyone who has read Holland (1975), a natural way to proceed is to represent an entire rule set as a string (an individual), maintain a population of candidate rule sets, and use selection and genetic operators to produce new generations of rule sets. Historically, this was the approach taken by De Jong and his students while at the University of Pittsburgh (e.g., see Smith, 1980, 1983), which gave rise to the phrase "the Pitt approach."

However, during the same time period, Holland developed a model of cognition (classifier systems) in which the members of the population are individual rules and a rule set is represented by the entire population (e.g., see Holland & Reitman, 1978; Booker, 1982). This quickly became known as "the Michigan approach" and initiated a friendly but provocative series of discussions concerning the strengths and weaknesses of the two approaches. Below we consider each framework in more detail.

5.2.1 The Pitt approach

If we adopt the view that each individual in a GA population represents an *entire* PS program, there are several issues that must be addressed. The first is the (by now familiar) choice of representation. The most immediate representation that comes to mind is to regard individual rules as genes and to view entire programs as strings of these genes. Crossover then serves to provide new combinations of rules and mutation provides new rules. However, notice that we have chosen a representation in which genes can take on many values. As discussed in the previous section on parameter modification, this can result in premature convergence when population sizes are typically 50-100. Since individuals represent entire PS programs, it is unlikely that one can afford to significantly increase the size of the population. Nor, as we have seen, does it help to increase the rate of mutation. Rather, we need to move toward an internal binary representation of the space of PS programs so that crossover is also involved in constructing new rules from parts of existing rules.

If we go directly to a binary representation, we must now exercise care that crossover and mutation are appropriate operators in the sense in that they produce new high-potential individuals from existing ones. The simplest way to guarantee this is to assume that all rules have a fixed-length, fixed-field format. Although this may seem restrictive in comparison with the flexibility and variability of OPS5 (Forgy, 1981) or MYCIN (Buchanan & Shortliffe, 1984) rules, it has proven to be quite adequate when working at a lower sensory level. At this level, one typically has a fixed number of detectors and effectors, so that condition-action rules quite naturally take the form of a fixed number of detector patterns to be matched, together with an action appropriate for those conditions. Many of the successful classifier systems rely on this assumption (Wilson, 1985; Goldberg, 1985).

However, it is not difficult to relax this assumption and allow more flexible rule sets without subverting the power of the genetic operators. One can achieve this by making the operators "representation sensitive," in the sense that they no longer make arbitrary changes to linear bit strings. Rather, one extends the internal representation to provide punctuation marks so that only meaningful changes occur. For example, if the crossover operator chooses to break one parent on a rule boundary, it also breaks the other parent on a rule boundary. Smith (1983) and Schaffer (1985) have used this approach successfully in their LS systems.

A second representation-related issue that arises in the Pitt approach involves the number of rules in each set. If we think of rule sets as programs or knowledge bases, it seems rather artificial to demand that all rule sets be the same size. Historically, however, all of the analytical results and most of the experimental work has assumed GAs that maintain populations of fixed-length strings.

One can adopt the same view using the Pitt approach and require all rule sets (strings) to have the same fixed length. This can be justified in terms of the advantages of having redundant copies of rules and having workspace within a rule set for new experimental building blocks without necessarily having to replace existing ones. However, Smith (1980) has extended many of the formal results on genetic algorithms to variable-length strings. He complemented these results with a GA implementation that maintained a population of variable-length strings and that efficiently generated variable-length rule sets for a variety of tasks. One interesting contribution of this work was a method for keeping down the size of the rule sets, based on a bonus for achieving the same level of performance with a shorter string.

With these issues resolved, GAs have been shown to be surprisingly effective in producing nontrivial rule sets for such diverse tasks as solving maze problems, playing poker, and classifying gaits. We direct the interested reader to Smith (1983) and Schaffer (1985) for more details.

5.2.2 The Michigan approach

Holland and his colleagues developed a quite different approach to learning production-system programs while working on computational models of cognition. In this context, it seemed natural to view the knowledge (experience) of a particular person (cognitive entity) as a collection of rules that are modified over time via interaction with the environment. Unlike genetic material, this kind of knowledge does not evolve over generations via selection and mating. Rather, it accumulates in real time as the individual struggles to cope with his environment. Out of this perspective came a family of cognitive models called *classifier systems*, in which *rules* rather than *rules sets* are the internal entities manipulated by genetic algorithms.

Classifier systems consist of a set of rules (*classifiers*) that manipulate an internal message list. The left-hand side of each classifier consists of a pattern that matches messages on the message list. The right-hand side of each classifier specifies a message to be posted on the message list if that classifier is allowed to fire. Interaction with the environment is achieved via a task-specific set of detectors that post detector messages on the message list, along with a set of task-specific effectors that generate external actions in response to posted messages. A classifier system is "perturbed" by the arrival of one or more detector messages indicating a change in the environment. This results in a sequence of rule firings as the contents of the message list changes, and it may result in one or more responses in the form of effector actions.

Learning in classifier systems is achieved by requiring that the environment provide intelligent feedback to the classifier system in the form of reward (punishment) whenever favorable (unfavorable) states are reached. Since an arbitrary number of rules can fire during the interval between two successive payoffs, a significant credit assignment problem arises in determining how payoff should be distributed. Holland (1986) has developed a "bucket brigade" mechanism for solving this problem. Based on a strong "service economy" metaphor, the bucket brigade distributes payoff (wealth) to those rules actively involved in sequences that result in rewards. Over time, wealthier rules become more likely to fire, since they are favored by the conflict-resolution mechanism.

As described, classifier systems are able to select useful subsets of rules from an existing rule set. However, additional behavioral improvements can be obtained by making changes to the rules as well. As the reader may have guessed, this is achieved by interpreting the wealth of individual rules as a measure of "fitness," and using genetic algorithms to select, recombine, and replace rules on the basis of their fitness.

There are a number of impressive examples of classifier systems that regulate gas flow through pipelines (Goldberg, 1985), control vision systems (Wilson, 1985), and infer Boolean functions (Wilson, 1987). Which approach is better, the Pitt or Michigan approach, in the sense of being more effective in evolving task programs? It is too early to answer this question or even to determine if the question is valid. The current popular view is that the classifier approach will prove to be most useful in an on-line, real-time environment in which radical changes in behavior cannot be tolerated, whereas the Pitt approach will be more useful for off-line environments in which more leisurely exploration and more radical behavioral changes are acceptable.

5.3 Architectural issues for production systems

So far we have focused on representation issues in an attempt to understand how GAs can be used to learn PS programs. The only constraint on production-system architectures that has emerged is that GAs are much more effective on PS programs that consist of unordered rules. In this section we summarize some additional implications that the use of GAs might have on the design of PS architectures.

5.3.1 The left-hand side of rules

Many of the rule-based expert system paradigms (e.g., MYCIN-like shells) and most traditional programming languages provide an IF-THEN format in which the left-hand side is a Boolean expression to be evaluated. This Boolean sublanguage can itself become quite syntactically complex and can raise many of the representational issues discussed earlier. In particular, variable-length expressions, varying types of operators and operands, and function invocations make it difficult to choose a representation and/or a set of genetic operators that produce useful offspring easily and efficiently.

Languages like OPS5 and SNOBOL take an alternative approach, assuming the left-hand side is a pattern to be matched. Unfortunately, the pattern language can be as complex as Boolean expressions and in some cases is even more complex, due to the additional need to save matched objects for later use in the pattern or in the right-hand side.

Consequently, the GA implementor must temper the style and complexity of the left-hand side with the need for an effective internal representation. As a consequence, many implementations have followed Holland's lead and have chosen the simple {0, 1, #} fixed-length pattern language, permitting a direct application of traditional genetic operators, which were designed to manipulate fixed-length binary strings. When combined with internal working memory, such languages can be shown to be computationally complete. However, this choice is not without problems. The rigid fixed-length nature of the patterns can require complex and creative representations of the objects to be matched. Simple relationships like "*speed* > 200" may require multiple rule firings and the use of internal memory to ensure correct evaluation. As discussed earlier, some of this rigidity can be alleviated by the use of context-sensitive genetic operators (Smith 1983). However, finding a better compromise between simplicity and expressive power of the left-hand sides is an active area of research.

A favorite psychological motivation for preferring pattern matching rather than Boolean expressions is the intuition that humans use the powerful mechanism of partial matching to deal with the enormous variety of every day life. Seldom are humans in precisely the same situation twice, but they manage to function reasonably well by noting the current situation's similarity to previous experience.

This has led to interesting discussions as to how GAs might capture similarity computationally in a natural and efficient way. Holland and other advocates of the {0, 1, #} paradigm argue that this is precisely the role that the wild-card symbol "#" plays as patterns evolve to their appropriate level of generality. Booker (1982, 1985) and others have suggested that requiring perfect matches *even* with the {0, 1, #} pattern language is still too rigid a requirement, particularly as the length of the left-hand side pattern increases. Rather than returning simply success or failure, they feel that the pattern matcher should return a score indicating how close the pattern came to matching. This is an important issue, and we need more work on methods for computing match scores in a reasonably general but computationally efficient manner. We direct the interested reader to Booker (1985) for more details.

5.3.2 Working memory

Another PS architectural issue revolves around the decision about whether to use "stimulus-response" production systems, in which left-hand sides only attend to external events and right-hand sides consist only of invocations of external effectors, or whether to use the more general OPS model, in which rules can also attend to elements in an internal working memory and make changes to that memory.

Arguments in favor of the latter approach observe that the addition of working memory provides a more powerful computational engine, which is frequently required with fixed-length rule formats. The strength of this argument can be weakened somewhat by noting that in some cases the external environment *itself* can be used as a working memory.

Arguments against including working memory generally fall along three lines: (1) the application does not need the additional generality and complexity; (2) concerns about bounding the number of internal actions before generating the next external action (i.e., the halting problem); or (3) the fact that most of the more traditional concept-learning work (e.g., Winston, 1975; Michalski, 1983) has focused on stimulus-response approaches.

Most GA implementations of working memory provide a restricted form of internal memory, namely, a fixed-format, bounded-capacity message list (Holland & Reitman, 1978; Booker, 1982). However, it is clear that there are many uses for both classes of architecture. The important point here is that this choice is not imposed by GAs themselves.

5.3.3 Parallelism in production systems

Another side benefit of PSs with working memory is that they can be easily extended to allow parallel rule firings (Thibadeau, Just, & Carpenter, 1982; Rosenbloom & Newell, 1987). In principle, the only time that serialization must occur is when an external effector is activated. Hence, permitting parallel firing of rules that invoke internal actions is a natural way to extend PS architectures in order to exploit the power of parallelism. Of course, the implementor must decide whether this power is appropriate for a particular application. What should be clear is that GAs can be applied equally well to parallel PS architectures, leaving the choice to the designer.

5.4 The role of feedback

In attempting to understand how GAs can be used to learn PS programs, we have discussed how such programs can be represented and what kinds of architectures can be used to exploit the power of GAs. In this section we focus on a third issue: the role of feedback.

Recall that one can view GAs as using an adaptive sampling strategy to search large, complex spaces. This sampling scheme is adaptive in the sense that feedback from current samples is used to bias subsequent sampling into regions with high expected performance. This means that, even if one has chosen a good representation and has selected an appropriate PS architecture, the effectiveness of GAs in learning PS programs will also depend on the usefulness of the information obtained via feedback. Since the designer typically has a good deal of freedom on this dimension, it is important that he select a feedback mechanism that facilitates this adaptive search strategy.

Fortunately, there is a family of feedback mechanisms which are both simple to use and which experience has shown to be very effective: *payoff functions*. This form of feedback uses a classical "reward and punishment" scheme, in which performance evaluation is expressed in terms of a payoff value. GAs can employ this information (almost) directly to bias the selection of parents used to produce new samples (offspring). Of course, not all payoff functions are equally suited for this role. A good function will provide useful information early in the search process to help focus attention. For example, a payoff function that is nearly always zero provides almost no information for directing the search process.

The Michigan and Pitt approaches differ somewhat in the way they obtain payoff. In classifier systems, the bucket brigade mechanism stands ready to distribute payoff to those *rules* which are deemed responsible for achieving that payoff. Because payoff is the currency of the bucket brigade economy, a good feedback mechanism will provide a relatively steady flow of payoff, rather than having long "dry spells." Wilson's (1985) "animat" environment is an excellent example of this style of payoff.

The situation is somewhat different in the Pitt approach, since the usual view of evaluation consists of injecting an individual PS program into the task subsystem and evaluating how well that program *as a whole* performs. This view leads to some interesting issues, such as whether to reward a program that performs a task as well as others but uses less space (rules) or time (rule firings). Smith (1980) found it useful to break up the payoff function into two components: a task-specific evaluation and a task-independent measure of the program itself. Although he combined these two components into a single payoff value, recent work by Schaffer (1985) suggests that it might be more effective to use a vector-valued payoff function in such situations.

We still have much to learn about the role of feedback, from both an analytical and an empirical point of view. Bethke (1980) has used Walsh transforms in formally analyzing the types of feedback information that are best suited for GA-style adaptive search. Recent experimental work by Grefenstette (1988) suggests one way to combine aspects of both the Michigan and Pitt approaches, employing a multilevel credit assignment strategy that assigns payoff to both rule sets and individual rules. This is an interesting idea that promises to generate a good deal of discussion, and it merits further attention.

5.5 The use of domain knowledge

Genetic algorithms are conventionally viewed as domain-independent search methods in that they can be applied with no knowledge of the space being searched. However, although no domain knowledge is required, there are ample opportunities to exploit domain knowledge if it is available. We have already seen some examples of how domain knowledge can be incorporated. A designer must select the space to be searched and the internal representation to be used by GAs. As discussed in the previous sections, such decisions require knowledge about both the problem domain and the characteristics of GAs. The choice of genetic operators is closely related to representation decisions, and a significant domain knowledge can also enter into their selection. Grefenstette et al. (1985) provide an excellent discussion of these issues.

A more direct example of domain knowledge involves the choice of the initial population used to start the search process. Although we have described the initial population as randomly selected, there is no reason to start with an empty slate if one has *a priori* information available that permits seeding the initial population with individuals known to have certain performance levels.

A third and more obvious way to exploit domain knowledge is by means of the feedback mechanism. As we have seen, the effectiveness of GAs depends on the usefulness of the feedback information provided. Even the simplest form of feedback (the payoff-only method) can and frequently does incorporate domain knowledge into an effective payoff function. More elaborate forms of feedback, such as the vector-valued strategies and multi-level feedback mechanisms discussed above, provide additional opportunities to incorporate domain-specific knowledge. Thus, in practice we see a variety of scenarios. ranging from the use of "vanilla" GAs with little or no domain-specific modifications to highly creative applications that incorporate a good deal of domain knowledge.

6. Summary and conclusions

We started this paper with the goal of understanding how genetic algorithms might be applied to machine learning problems. We suggested that a good way to answer this question was to visualize a system as consisting of two components: a task subsystem whose behavior is to be modified over time via learning, and a learning subsystem responsible for observing the task subsystem over time and effecting the desired behavioral changes. This perspective let us focus on the kinds of *structural* changes a learning subsystem might make to a task subsystem in order to effect *behavioral* changes. We identified three classes of structural changes of increasing complexity: parameter modification, data structure manipulation, and changes to executable code.

Having characterized learning in this way, we restated the problem in terms of searching the space of legal structural changes for instances that achieve the desired behavioral changes. If one is working in a domain for which there is a strong theory to guide this search, it would be silly not to exploit such knowledge. However, there are many domains in which uncertainty and ignorance preclude such approaches and require the learning algorithm to discover (infer) the important characteristics of the search space *while* the search is in progress. This is the context in which GAs are most effective. Without requiring significant amounts of domain knowledge, GAs have been used to effectively search spaces from each of the categories listed above.

At the same time, it is important to understand the limitations of this approach. We have seen that in most cases 500–1000 samples must be taken from the search space before high-quality solutions are found. Clearly, there are many domains in which such a large number of samples is out of the question. We have also seen that the difficulty of choosing a good internal representation for the space increases with the complexity of the search space. Similarly, care must be taken to provide an effective feedback mechanism.

Thus, genetic algorithms are best viewed as another tool for the designer of learning systems. Like the more familiar inductive techniques and explanation-based methods, GA is not the answer to all learning problems, but it provides an effective strategy for specific types of situations.

Acknowledgements

I would like to thank the editors of this issue, David Goldberg and John Holland, for useful comments on an earlier draft of the paper.

References

Bethke, A. (1980). *Genetic algorithms as function optimizers.* Doctoral dissertation, Department of Computer and Communications Sciences, University of Michigan, Ann Arbor.

Booker, L. B. (1982). *Intelligent behavior as an adaptation to the task environment.* Doctoral dissertation, Department of Computer and Communications Sciences, University of Michigan, Ann Arbor.

Booker, L. B. (1985). Improving the performance of genetic algorithms in classifier systems. *Proceedings of the First International Conference on Genetic Algorithms and Their Applications* (pp. 80–92). Pittsburgh, PA: Lawrence Erlbaum.

Brindle, A. (1980). *Genetic algorithms for function optimization.* Doctoral dissertation, Department of Computing Science, University of Alberta, Edmonton, Alberta, Canada.

Buchanan, B. G., & Mitchell, T. M. (1978). Model-directed learning of production rules. In D. Waterman and F. Hayes-Roth (Eds.), *Pattern-directed inference systems.* New York: Academic Press.

Buchanan, B. G., & Shortliffe, E. A. (Eds.). (1984). *Rule-based expert systems.* Reading, MA: Addison-Wesley.

Davis, L. (1985). Job shop scheduling with genetic algorithms. *Proceedings of the First International Conference on Genetic Algorithms and Their Applications* (pp. 136–140). Pittsburgh, PA: Lawrence Erlbaum.

De Jong, K. A. (1975). *An analysis of the behavior of a class of genetic adaptive systems.* Doctoral dissertation, Department of Computer and Communications Sciences, University of Michigan, Ann Arbor.

De Jong, K. (1980). Adaptive system design: A genetic approach. *IEEE Transactions on Systems, Man, and Cybernetics, 10,* 556–574.

De Jong, K. (1985). Genetic algorithms: A 10 year perspective. *Proceedings of the First International Conference on Genetic Algorithms and Their Applications* (pp. 169–177). Pittsburgh, PA: Lawrence Erlbaum.

Fisher, D. H. (1987). Knowledge acquisition via incremental conceptual clustering. *Machine Learning, 2,* 139–172.

Forgy, C. L. (1981). OPS5 *user's manual* (Technical Report CMU-CS-81-135). Pittsburgh, PA: Carnegie Mellon University, Department of Computer Science.

Fujiki, C., & Dickinson, J. (1987). Using the genetic algorithm to generate LISP source code to solve the prisoner's dilemma. *Genetic Algorithms and Their Applications: Proceedings of the Second International Conference on Genetic Algorithms* (pp. 236–240). Cambridge, MA: Lawrence Erlbaum.

Goldberg, D. E. (1985). Genetic algorithms and rule learning in dynamic system control. *Proceedings of the First International Conference on Genetic Algorithms and Their Applications* (pp. 8–15). Pittsburgh, PA: Lawrence Erlbaum.

Goldberg, D. E., & Lingle, R. (1985). Alleles, loci, and the traveling salesman problem. *Proceedings of the First International Conference on Genetic Algorithms and Their Applications* (pp. 154–159). Pittsburgh, PA: Lawrence Erlbaum.

Grefenstette, J. (1986). Optimization of control parameters for genetic algorithms. *IEEE Transactions on Systems, Man, and Cybernetics, 16,* 122–128.

Grefenstette, J. J. (1988). Credit assignment in rule discovery systems based on genetic algorithms. *Machine Learning, 3,* 225–245.

Grefenstette, J., Gopal, R., Rosmaita, B., & Van Gucht, D. (1985). Genetic algorithms for the traveling salesman problem. *Proceedings of the First International Conference on Genetic Algorithms and their Applications* (pp. 160–168). Pittsburgh, PA: Lawrence Erlbaum.

Hedrick, C. L. (1976). Learning production systems from examples. *Artificial Intelligence, 7,* 21–49.

Holland, J. H. (1975). *Adaptation in natural and artificial systems.* Ann Arbor, MI: University of Michigan Press.

Holland J. H. (1986). Escaping brittleness: The possibilities of general-purpose learning algorithms applied to parallel rule-based systems. In R. S. Michalski, J. G. Carbonell, & T. M. Mitchell (Eds.), *Machine learning: An artificial intelligence approach* (Vol. 2). Los Altos, CA: Morgan Kaufmann.

Holland, J. H., & Reitman, J. S. (1978). Cognitive systems based on adaptive algorithms. In D. A. Waterman & F. Hayes-Roth (Eds.), *Pattern-directed inference systems.* New York: Academic Press.

Michalski, R. S. (1983). A theory and methodology of inductive learning. In R. S. Michalski, J. G. Carbonell, & T. M. Mitchell (Eds.), *Machine learning: An artificial intelligence approach.* Los Altos, CA: Morgan Kaufmann.

Neches, R., Langley, P., & Klahr, D. (1987). Learning, development, and production systems. In D. Klahr, P. Langley, & R. Neches (Eds.), *Production system models of learning and development.* Cambridge, MA: MIT Press.

Newell, A. (1973). Production systems: Models of control structures. In W. G. Chase (Ed.), *Visual information processing.* New York: Academic Press.

Rosenbloom, P., & Newell, A. (1987). Learning by chunking: A production system model of practice. In D. Klahr, P. Langley, & R. Neches (Eds.), *Production system models of learning and development.* Cambridge, MA: MIT Press.

Samuel, A. L. (1959). Some studies of machine learning using the game of checkers. *IBM Journal of Research and Development, 3,* 210–229.

Samuel, A. L. (1967). Some studies of machine learning using the game of checkers, II – Recent progress. *IBM Journal of Research and Development, 11,* 601–617.

Schaffer, J. D. (1985). Multiple objective optimization with vector evaluated genetic algorithms. *Proceedings of the First International Conference on Genetic Algorithms and Their Applications* (pp. 93–100). Pittsburgh, PA: Lawrence Erlbaum.

Smith, S. F. (1980). *A learning system based on genetic adaptive algorithms.* Doctoral dissertation, Department of Computer Science, University of Pittsburgh, PA.

Smith, S. F. (1983). Flexible learning of problem solving heuristics through adaptive search. *Proceedings of the Eighth International Joint Conference on Artificial Intelligence* (pp. 422–425). Karlsruhe, West Germany: Morgan Kaufmann.

Thibadeau, R., Just, M., & Carpenter, P. (1982). A model of the time course and content of reading. *Cognitive Science, 6,* 157–203.

Wilson, S. W. (1985). Knowledge growth in an artificial animal. *Proceedings of the First International Conference on Genetic Algorithms and Their Applications* (pp. 16–23). Pittsburgh, PA: Lawrence Erlbaum.

Wilson, S. W. (1987). Quasi-Darwinian learning in a classifier system. *Proceedings of the Fourth International Workshop on Machine Learning* (pp. 59–65). Irvine, CA: Morgan Kaufmann.

Winston, P. H. (1975). Learning structural descriptions from examples. In P. H. Winston (Ed.), *The psychology of computer vision.* New York: McGraw-Hill.

ESCAPING BRITTLENESS:

The Possibilities of General-Purpose Learning Algorithms Applied to Parallel Rule–Based Systems

John H. Holland
University of Michigan

Abstract

Message-passing, rule-based production systems in which many rules are active simultaneously offer attractive possibilities for the exploitation of general-purpose machine learning algorithms. In such systems each rule can be looked upon as a tentative hypothesis about some aspect of the task environment, competing against other plausible hypotheses being entertained at the same time. In this context there are two major tasks for machine learning algorithms: (1) apportionment of credit and (2) rule discovery.

The apportionment-of-credit algorithm(s) must assign "strength" to rules on the basis of their observed usefulness to the system. The problem is complicated by the difficulty of determining which of a cluster of rules active in an early, "stage-setting" capacity has contributed to a later useful outcome (e.g., rules controlling early moves that make possible a later triple jump in checkers). If strengths can be assigned appropriately, then they can be used to determine a rule's ability to win against competing rules, and they can be used to determine the rule's likelihood of being used as a "parent" for new rules. Surprisingly, for credit apportionment algorithms of the *bucket-brigade* variety, one can prove fixed-point theorems that provide some guarantees of an appropriate apportionment.

The task of rule discovery depends critically upon the discovery of good "building blocks" for generating plausible rules (hypotheses). A parallel system designed with machine learning in mind must permit a constant flux of new rules to be tested and exploited or discarded. Moreover this flux must not disturb the system's behavior in task environments for which it has well-practiced, effective procedures. *Genetic algorithms,* using the strengths as "fitnesses," offer subtle ways of discovering good building blocks, and there are new versions of theorems from mathematical genetics that enable us to understand this discovery process.

20.1 INTRODUCTION

The research that has culminated in the design of expert systems is a solid achievement for artificial intelligence: Given appropriately restricted domains, expert systems display the reasoned consideration of alternatives that one expects of an expert. The source of this success, the domain-specific character of the systems, is also a source of limitations. The systems are *brittle* in the sense that they respond appropriately only in narrow domains and require substantial human intervention to compensate for even slight shifts in domain (see Duda and Shortliffe, 1983). This problem of brittleness and ways to temper it are the main concern of this chapter. The overall theme is that *induction* is the basic—and perhaps only—way of making large advances in this direction.

To gain a clearer idea of the scope of the overall problem, consider some of the specific problems induction faces in this context. At the top of the list is the task of generating useful ways of categorizing input. In complex domains there is a perpetual novelty to the input so that experience can guide future action only if the system discovers regularities or recurrences in the input. The categories induced must be broad enough to "cover" the likely possibilities parsimoniously; at the same time they must be specific enough to distinguish situations requiring different behaviors. Categories must be incorporated into rules that "point" both to actions and to an aura of associated categories. That is, as the categories are induced, they must be arranged in a "tangled hierarchy" (see Fahlman, 1979) that enables the system to model its environment appropriately.

On a larger scale induction must provide plausible alternatives and changes in the hierarchies and models based upon these categories. In this structure, credit must be apportioned to the all-important categories that point to "stage-setting" actions necessary for later success. Because of the uncertainty of any induction, the process must be carried out in such a way that the system can absorb new, tentative rules without destroying capabilities in well-practiced situations. In all but the simplest situations a complex combination of competing rules will be activated so that the system must select a subset of rules that provides a coherent "picture" (model) of the situation. This picture in turn directs behavior and attempts at confirmation. At the highest level, the system must make effective use of metaphor and analogy to transfer inferences from familiar to unfamiliar situations (a capacity only touched upon in this chapter). The first two sections of the chapter will expand upon these problems.

Section 20.2 takes a closer look at the notions of domain and environment, and section 20.3 examines (informal) criteria bearing on the escape from brittleness.

The approach advocated in this chapter is based upon a class of message-passing, rule-based systems, called *classifier systems,* in which large numbers of rules can be active simultaneously. Individual rules can be kept simple and standardized because combinations of rules are used to define complex situations. This approach results in both parsimony and flexibility, because the same rule can be used in many contexts (see criterion 1 in section 20.3). Moreover, it gives a different slant to the induction task—the object becomes that of finding rules that serve well in a variety of tasks.

All rules are in condition/action form. Each condition specifies the set of messages satisfying it, and each action specifies the message sent when the condition part is satisfied. Because messages are kept to a standard length, it is possible to define conditions using strings of standard length, and this is done in such a way that it is simple to set the generality of a condition. As a consequence default hierarchies are easy to generate and use. Rules can be tied together into networks of various kinds by appropriate use of tagging. Section 20.4 describes classifier systems in detail.

Simplicity of the component rules also eases the tasks of the learning algorithms. First among these tasks is that of rating the usefulness of existing rules. This is the task of the *bucket-brigade* algorithm; it assigns a *strength* to each individual rule, modifying the strength on the basis of the rule's overall usefulness as the system accumulates experience. In effect the algorithm treats each rule as a middleman in a complex economy, its survival being dependent upon "making a profit" in its local interactions. In the long run, such profits will recur only if the rule is tied into chains of interactions leading to successful actions. Bucket-brigade algorithms are defined and described in the first part of section 20.5.

The most difficult inductive task is that of generating plausible new rules. Here that task is carried out by a *genetic algorithm.* It uses high-strength classifiers as the "parents" of new classifiers to be tested under the bucket brigade. Although the genetic algorithm acts directly upon the strings defining classifiers, it can be shown that it is implicitly searching and using a space of "building blocks." Moreover, it is searching this space orders of magnitude more rapidly than would be indicated by the rate at which it is processing strings. Rules generated by the genetic algorithm do not displace their parents; rather they displace low-strength rules, entering into competition with the other rules in the system. This competition gives the overall system a graceful way of handling conflicts and tentative hypotheses. The latter part of section 20.5 describes genetic algorithms and their effects upon classifiers.

Systems organized along these lines have been tested successfully in a variety of contexts. For example, a poker-playing version of the system (Smith, 1980), starting with classifiers embodying only the rules of the game, competed with overwhelming success against Waterman's learning poker player (Waterman and Hayes-Roth, 1978). Recently Goldberg (1983) tested a system that, starting with a clean slate (randomly generated classifiers), confronted a gas pipeline transmission problem involving diurnal variation, seasonal variation, and leaks. The system generated successful control procedures embedded in a (discovered) default hierarchy distinguishing normal operation from "leaky" operation. Additional tests are discussed in section 20.6.

20.2 DOMAINS AND ENVIRONMENTS

A closer look at the role of induction begins with a closer look at the domains—the *environment*—in which the system is to operate. The environment provides the grist for the inductive mill, thereby setting the possibilities for, and the ultimate limitations on, the inductive process. An environment with no regularities (however defined) offers no opportunities for induction. Human experience indicates that real environments abound in regularities. The problem is to uncover and exploit them.

This chapter will restrict itself to environments that, implicitly or explicitly, present problems in terms of goals to be attained. In this context the system "closes the loop" through the environment, receiving information from the environment and acting upon the environment to bring about changes therein. The environment signals the solution of a problem by feeding back a quantity called *payoff*. (This term from game theory, chosen for its neutrality, is the cognate of *utility* in economics, *error signals* in control theory, *fitness* in genetics, *reward* in psychology, and so on.) This format cleanly exposes most of the difficult problems in planning and problem solving, ranging from game playing though the design of mobile robots to abstract tasks such as the production of a corpus of useful theorems. The system uses the states of the environment as "stepping stones" to reach goal states that feed back payoff. The problem, simply, is to go efficiently from "here," a nongoal state, to "there," a goal state. The subtleties underlying this simple statement increase rapidly as the complexity of the state graph of the environment increases. One need go no further than the game trees and simply defined goals of chess or go to see deep subtleties; real-world situations typified by the design of flexible robots or interactive information retrieval systems offer even deeper problems.

The system can be thought of as receiving information about the current state of its environment in the form of *messages* generated by an input interface. The input interface typically consists of a set of feature detectors, and the message consists of a string of feature values. The systems dealt with here generally do *not* have high-level interpreters for these messages. That is, the rules of the system work directly on the message strings, acting on the presence or absence of certain bits. Whatever meanings there are, are supplied by the actions of the rules and, ultimately, by the effects produced on the environment.

The contrast between this "environment-oriented" approach and a "language-oriented" approach is worth pointing up. Consider the game of checkers. A language-oriented approach would use a language (symbols, grammar, etc., based, say, on standard checkers move notation) to specify legal moves, desirable configurations, and so on. The language, with an interpreter providing properties of board configurations and the like, would then be used, along with deductive inference, to develop a goal-oriented plan. The environment-oriented approach uses detectors (cf. the "parameters" used by Samuel, 1959) to generate bit strings based on the checkerboard configuration. These messages are processed by rules (arranged in a complex default hierarchy; see below) to determine plans and moves. An environment-oriented approach does not explicitly assign abstract symbols to board configurations, nor does it explicitly search for and apply grammatical rules to such symbols.

Note that the environment-oriented approach is *not* more restricted in its powers of definition than the language-oriented approach. The ultimate limits on the definitional powers of either approach are set by the input interface. The system cannot distinguish environmental state configurations assigned identical values by the input interface, be they symbols or feature strings. (This sets aside certain sequential tests, but the argument remains the same even if these are used. More formally, the input interface groups environmental states into equivalence classes; elements of the same equivalence class are the same as far as the system is concerned.) All that definition can do under either approach is to categorize the distinguishable. It divides the distinguishable elements into two classes—those that satisfy the definition and those that do not.

If the system is computationally complete (can define any procedure) with respect to sorting the input messages into classes, then it has reached the limits of what definition can do for it relative to distinguishability. Stated another way, if two systems are computationally complete with respect to input interfaces that set identical restrictions on distinguishability, then the systems have the same limits on their powers of definition. This is true even if one system is language-oriented and the other is environment-oriented. The environment-oriented systems that will be examined shortly accomplish definition by a combination of conditions, tags, and recoding (see section 20.4.3); they are computationally complete relative to the set of messages produced by any input interface.

20.3 CRITERIA

This investigation of ways of avoiding brittleness has been guided by several informal criteria derived primarily from ruminations about flexible natural systems and consideration of various landmarks in machine learning. The systems defined in the next section are intended as procedural implementations of these criteria, which are as follows:

1. Recombination and parallelism. In order to avoid a distinct rule for each situation (a "visiting grandmother" rule, a "yellow Volkswagon with a flat tire" rule, etc.), it is imperative that the system's response to any situation be mediated by the concurrent activation of a *set* of relevant rules. By activating several elementary rules in response to a complex set of conditions, rather than relying on anticipation of the overall situation by provision of a single preformed rule, the system sets combinatorics to work for it rather than against it. As a simple example, by selecting one each from ten hairlines, ten eye configurations, ten noses, ten mouths, and ten jawlines, the system can match any one of one hundred thousand distinct faces at the cost of retaining only fifty elementary rules. Under this criterion, it is incumbent upon induction and learning to search for rules that are useful "building blocks" in a variety of contexts. If the building blocks are well chosen, the system may be able to function well in situations not previously encountered. For instance, if the system has rules categorizing and handling input messages according to the usual notions of *hooved, four-legged,* and *horned,* it is conceivable that it would infer that a unicorn (observed for the first time) is *herbivorous.*

2. Categorization and default hierarchies. Categorization is the system's major weapon for combating the environment's perpetual novelty. The system must readily generate categories for input messages, and it must be able to generate categories relevant to its internal processes. These candidates must be tested repeatedly for usefulness and used with increasing or decreasing frequency in accord with the outcome (see criterion 5, "Competition, confirmation, and gracefulness," below).

Moreover, there must be some criterion of plausibility so that the system is not overwhelmed with poor candidates. Appropriate bottom-up procedures (e.g., generalization of input messages) and top-down procedures (e.g., recombination of parts of the definitions of extant categories) can go far toward implementing this constraint. The categories generated should spontaneously arrange themselves into a default hierarchy (much like the skeleton of Fahlman's NETL, 1979), so that details invoke "sketches" of the situations, allowing transfer of information between experiences activating similar sketches. (The more rules held in common by the clusters of rules defining two sketches, the more similar they are.) High-level interpreters for determining categories should be avoided where possible because they impose complex relations between syntax and semantics, greatly complicating the induction of categories.

3. Association. The use of categories as building blocks is much enhanced if, as the categories develop, an aura of associations with other categories also develops. Various "triggers," such as the co-occurrence of a pair of categories in a given environmental situation, can limit the formation of associations to plausible candidates. Associations are recorded by *synchronic pointers*—pointers that do *not* imply temporal sequence—and these pointers must be tested repeatedly for usefulness (see criterion 5). The generation and selection of the categories and pointers that serve as building blocks are processes that provide the system with a wide range of structures that act much like *virtual copies* (Fahlman, 1979). To use a biological analogy, these virtual copies play the role of "species" filling the "niches" defined by the regularities (opportunities for exploitation) uncovered in the system's experience. The meaning of the virtual copies stems from the process of competition and selection that determines their emergence. This contrasts strongly with attempts to arrive at such structures a priori, which is much like attempting to develop a taxonomy for species without understanding their ontogeny.

4. Diachronic pointing, models, and prediction. Although Samuel's paper (1959) is often cited in machine learning, his use of model building to solve problems is almost always overlooked. (This may be because he modeled strategies by using linear forms, forms that typically serve only as linear pattern recognition devices.) Because of the model building, Samuel's checkers player can refine its strategy while playing the game, when there is no payoff from the environment. This greatly enhances the system's flexibility. When a system uses a model to generate expectations or predictions, it can use subsequent verification or falsification of the predictions to guide revisions of the model (toward better prediction) even in the absence of payoff.

In the present context, the construction of a model requires that the system include a second kind of pointer—the *diachronic pointers*—to indicate temporal sequences of categories. In short, the system forms temporal associations. Trigger conditions serve to restrict the generation of candidates, as they did in the case of synchronic pointers. For example, if a well-established category Y consistently follows well-established category X when the system makes response R, then it is plausible to induce a diachronic pointer between X and Y. (Note that a general category will often describe an environmental situation that persists over an extended period, as in the case of a *going home* or *pursuit of prey* category, allowing the trigger to link categories well separated in time.) As in the case of synchronic pointers, the diachronic pointers must be subjected to continued selection for usefulness.

5. Competition, confirmation, and gracefulness. The previous criteria have exploited parallelism to provide clusters of rules that serve both as virtual copies and as models. Parallelism neatly sidesteps the priority issues of one-rule-at-a-time systems but leaves open questions concerning conflict and consistency. Of all the elementary rules that are candidates for activation in a given situation, which ones get the nod?

The foundation for an answer is set by an effective apportionment-of-credit algorithm. Strengths must be assigned to rules in accord with their past usefulness in the situations in which they have been invoked. Once again Samuel (1959) leads the way. The problem is one of strengthening stage-setting rules that make possible later actions yielding payoff. The exploitation of predictions provides a mechanism. Let us assume, following Samuel, that the strength of a rule amounts to a prediction of the average payoff the system will receive *later* if the rule is invoked *concurrently* as part of a cluster. Assume further that a second rule is coupled to the given rule by a diachronic pointer. If this second rule has a strength (prediction) very different from that of the first rule, then the strength of the first rule can be revised to bring it into line with the later prediction (see discussion in Samuel, 1959, and the definition of the bucket-brigade algorithm in section 20.5). When the system has such an algorithm for revising strengths, then the invocation of rules can be decided by a competition based on strength and the degree to which the rule's conditions are satisfied by the current situation.

In effect the various rules held by the system are treated as competing hypotheses. The winners are the system's estimate of the current situation. It is critical to the system's performance and flexibility that its rules represent a wide range of competing, even conflicting, hypotheses. The competition replaces a criterion of global consistency—a criterion that is infeasible for any very large system of rules—with one of progressive confirmation under the apportionment-of-credit algorithm. With this outlook, rules that consistently make poor predictions when invoked have their strength steadily decreased to the point that they are displaced by newer candidates. The newer candidates must in turn compete, usually doing well in "niches" not well handled by rules already in the system. The combination of competition and confirmation contributes to the system's *gracefulness:* Large numbers of new candidates can be injected without disturbing performance in well-practiced domains.

20.4 CLASSIFIER SYSTEMS

20.4.1 Overview

Classifier systems are general-purpose programming systems designed to meet the objectives and criteria set forth in sections 20.2 and 20.3. They have been designed from the outset to be amenable to modification by learning algorithms. Particular attention has been given to questions of gracefulness and to the provision of "natural" building blocks. The systems have already been tested in a variety of contexts (see section 20.6).

Classifier systems have many affinities to the rule-based (production system) approach to expert systems (see, for example, Davis and King, 1977, or Waterman and Hayes-Roth, 1978) but with the following major differences:

1. Any number of rules, called *classifiers,* can be active at the same time. There can be no direct conflict between classifiers because the only action of a classifier is to post a message to a global message list—the more classifiers activated, the more messages on the message list. The resulting conflict-free concurrency sidesteps the difficult conflict resolution problems of one-rule-at-a-time systems (see McDermott and Forgy, 1978), allowing the system to use many rules concurrently to summarize and act upon a situation. The rules become building

blocks that can be combined to handle a wide variety of situations. Moreover, the parallelism makes it easier to specify and control the parallel processes that pervade the real world.

2. Messages are strings of fixed length k over a fixed alphabet, taken to be $\{1,0\}$ in the definitions that follow. Classifiers, as is usual with production systems, consist of a *condition* part and an *action* part, but the conditions are all specified by strings of length k over the alphabet $\{1,0,\#\}$. With this provision it is possible to use a simple matching operator to test whether or not some message satisfies a condition. From the architectural viewpoint, the fixed lengths encourage organizations exploiting fixed-length registers, an important consideration in simulations or physical realizations.

3. When the condition part of a classifier is satisfied by some message on the message list, the action part uses the message to form a new message, which is posted on the new message list. Thus the basic procedure of the *system* is a simple loop in which all classifiers access the current message list, determine if their conditions have been satisfied, and if so, post messages to the message list for the next time-step. As mentioned earlier, any number of classifiers can be active simultaneously without conflict, because actions only add messages to the new message list.

4. All external communication (input and output) is via messages to the message list. As a result, all internal control information and external communication reside in the same data structure.

5. Because the order in which classifiers are executed is independent of the order in which the classifiers are stored, and because satisfaction of conditions is determined by a simple matching operation, there is no need for an interpreter. This makes it possible to design local syntactic operators that modify systems of classifiers ("programs") in useful ways, something difficult to do for standard languages or production systems but very important if the system is to be modified by learning algorithms or expert advice.

6. Because of the global nature of the message list, tagging and related techniques become efficient ways of "coupling" classifiers, forcing predetermined execution sequences, and so on. The combination of concurrency and a global list avoids the limitations on tagging discussed by Davis and King (1977) in their review of production systems.

20.4.2 Definition of the Basic Elements: Classifiers and Messages

Classifiers have the same role in classifier systems that instructions have in computer language. They are called classifiers because they can be used to classify messages into general sets, but they are broader in concept and application than this name would indicate, providing both processing and recoding. The message specified by the action part of the classifier changes the internal state of the system, thereby influencing later action, and it may cause external (effector) action. Provided with some simple message-processing capabilities, classifiers can carry out arbitrary operations on messages, including recursions. It follows that there are classifier systems that are computationally universal.

The major technical hurdle in implementing a message-processing version of a production system is that of providing a simple way of defining conditions in terms of messages. Each condition specifies a subset of the set of all possible messages—the set of messages that *satisfies* the condition. There is no simple and compact way of specifying an arbitrary subset of a large set; that is, most subsets must be specified element by element. Nevertheless there is one large and important class of subsets that *can* be simply specified, and any other subset can be defined as a union of these subsets. Each subset in this special class is specified by a string of length k over the three-letter alphabet $\{1,0,\#\}$. (Recall that messages, for present purposes, are strings of length k over the alphabet $\{1,0\}$.) The $\#$ symbol plays the role here of a "don't care" in the sense that wherever a $\#$ occurs in the specifying string one can substitute either a 1 or a 0 and still have a member of the subset. For example, the string $11 \ldots 1\#$ specifies the subset of exactly two elements, namely, the messages $\{11 \ldots 11, 11 \ldots 10\}$, and the string $1\#\# \ldots \#\#$ specifies the subset consisting of all messages that start with a 1.

More formally, let

$$\langle s_1, s_2, \ldots, s_j, \ldots s_k \rangle, \quad s_j \in \{1,0,\#\}$$

be a string of k symbols specifying a subset, and let

$$\langle m_1, m_2, \ldots, m_k \rangle, \quad m_j \in \{1,0\}$$

be a k-bit message. The message belongs to the specified subset just in case

1. if $s_j = 1$ or $s_j = 0$, then $m_j = s_j$
2. if $s_j = \#$, then m_j can be either 1 or 0.

The subset consists of all messages satisfying this requirement; that is, each subset is a hyperplane in the space of messages.

In this notation, classifier conditions are specified using strings of length k over the alphabet $\{1,0,\#\}$. We extend the notation by allowing the string to be prefixed by a minus sign $(-)$, with the intended interpretation that the prefixed condition is satisfied only if *no* message of the given subset is present on the message list. That is, if string c specifies subset S of the set of all messages, the condition $-c$ is *not* satisfied just in case the message list contains a message belonging to S. Combinations of classifiers can be used to implement conditions over arbitrary subsets in much the same way that AND, OR, and NOT can be combined to yield arbitrary Boolean functions (see section 20.4.3).

When the condition part of a classifier is satisfied, it produces a message specified by its action (or message specification) part. The action part, like the condition part, is specified by a string of length k that contains the # symbol, but the # has a different meaning. Now it plays the role of a "pass through" in the sense that wherever the # symbol occurs in the action part, the corresponding bit in a message satisfying the condition part is passed through into the outgoing message. For example, consider the message specification $11 \ldots 1\#$ in the action part of the classifier, and assume the message $00 \ldots 00$ satisfies the condition part of the classifier. Then the outgoing message will be $11 \ldots 10$.

More formally, let

$$\langle a_1, a_2, \ldots, a_j, \ldots a_k \rangle, \quad a_j \in \{1,0,\#\}$$

be a string of k symbols in the action part of a classifier, and let

$$\langle m_1, m_2, \ldots, m_j, \ldots, m_k \rangle, \quad m_j \in \{1,0\}$$

be a message satisfying the condition part of the classifier. Then the outgoing message, at position j, has value

1. a_j, if $a_j = 1$ or 0
2. m_j, if $a_j = \#$.

In brief, if a message satisfies the condition of a classifier, a new message is generated from the action portion of the classifier by using the 1's and 0's of the action part and passing through bits of the satisfying message at the pass through positions of the action part.

It is useful to generalize the notion of a classifier to allow an arbitrary number of conditions. Condition i of an r-condition classifier C is specified by a string c_i of length k over the symbols $\{1,0,\#\}$, possibly prefixed by a $-$; the action part is specified by a single string a of a length k over the symbols $\{1,0,\#\}$. Notationally, the conditions in the condition part are separated by "," and the action part is separated from the condition part by "/". Thus the specification of an r-condition classifier will have the form

$$c_1, c_2, \ldots, c_r/a.$$

The condition part of the classifier C is *satisfied* if each condition c_i is satisfied by some message M_j on the current message list. When the classifier is satisfied, an outgoing message M^* is generated as before using the message M_j satisfying condition c_1 and the action part a. At each position where a has a bit 0 or 1, M^* gets that bit; at each position where a has a pass through #, M^* gets the corresponding bit of M_j.

These definitions are sufficient to define the basic elements of a classifier system. A *classifier system* consists of a list of classifiers $\{C_1, C_2, \ldots, C_N\}$, a message list, an input interface, and an output interface. The *basic execution cycle* of this system proceeds as follows:

1. Place all messages from the input interface on the current message list.
2. Compare all messages to all conditions and record all matches.
3. For each match generate a message for the new message list.
4. Replace the current message list by the new message list.
5. Process the new message list through the output interface to produce system output.
6. Return to step 1.

A classifier system may be augmented by algorithms for "look-ahead," inference, and learning. Several methods for doing these things will be described in the next two subsections and in section 20.5. For some of these, weights are associated with classifiers and messages, and wherever a match is made a record is kept of the classifier that is satisfied and of the combinations of messages that satisfied it so that these weights can be modified periodically. Such enriched systems will still be called classifier systems unless there is some distinction to be pointed up by using a different name.

Because matching messages against conditions is a simple process, the central loop of the process (step 2 above) proceeds rapidly even on standard von Neumann architectures. One simulation currently in operation executes a time-step involving 256 conditions and thirty-two messages in less than 0.1 second. Parallel architectures offer speedups in proportion to the parallelism.

20.4.3 Tagging and Networks

Pointers, action sequences, and other processes dependent upon "addressing" are attained using *tags* to *couple* classifiers.

A classifier C_2 is coupled to a classifier C_1 if some condition of C_2 is satisfied by the message(s) generated by the action part of C_1. Note that a classifier with very specific conditions (few #'s) will typically be coupled to only a few other classifiers, and a classifier with very general conditions (many #'s) will be coupled to many other classifiers. When used to implement part of a "semantic network" or neural network, a classifier with very specific conditions has few incoming branches, and a classifier with very general conditions has many incoming branches.

Tags are a simple way of providing coupling. For example, any message with the prefix 1101 will satisfy a condition of the form 1101# . . . #, so a classifier with this condition in effect has an address: to send a message to this classifier one employs the prefix 1101. Since b bits yield 2^b tags and tags can be placed anywhere in a condition, a great number of conditions can be addressed uniquely.

By using appropriate prefixes, one can define a classifier that attends to a specific set of classifiers. Consider a pair of classifiers C_1 and C_2 that send messages tagged with 1101 and 1001, respectively. A classifier with the condition 1101## . . . ## will attend only to C_1, whereas a classifier with the configuration 1#01## . . . ## will attend to both C_1 and C_2. Using a combination of pass throughs (#'s in the action parts) and recodings (in which the prefix on the outgoing message differs from that of the satisfying messages), one can circumvent, usually with little effort, the limitation that the conditions be hyperplanes in the message space.

Boolean compounds of conditions—and hence the specification of conditions satisfied by arbitrarily chosen subsets of messages—are readily achieved by tags. An AND-condition is expressed by a single multicondition classifier such as $M_1, M_2/M$, for M is only added to the list if *both M_1 and M_2* are satisfied. An OR-condition is expressed by a set of classifiers such as $\{M_1/M; M_2/M\}$, for M is added to the list if *either M_1 or M_2* is satisfied. With these primitives, any Boolean form can be expressed by a set of classifiers. For example,

$$(M_1 \ \& \ M_2) \ \lor \ [(M_3 \ \& \ (-M_4)]$$

is achieved by the classifiers

$$\{M_1, M_2/M_5 \ ; \ M_3, -M_4/M_5\}.$$

The judicious use of #'s and recoding again reduces the number of classifiers required when the Boolean expressions are complex. By assigning tags to the input, internal, and output states of a finite system, one can realize arbitrary state transition diagrams.

The use of tags to couple classifiers for purposes of control and sequencing is illustrated in detail in the next subsection. The example also illustrates the use of concurrency and distributed control in classifier systems.

20.4.4 A Simple Classifier Control System

Figure 20-1 gives the schematic of a simple control routine for a classifier system operating in a two-dimensional environment. When there is an object of a specified type anywhere in the system's field of vision, this classifier routine acts to bring the system next to the object and hold it there.

The environment contains objects distributed over a planar surface. The input interface produces a message for an object in the field of vision. This message indicates the relative position of the object in the field of vision (left-of-center, center, right-of-center) and whether it is distant from or adjacent to the system. The classifiers process this information and issue commands to the output interface (ROTATE VISION VECTOR [LEFT, RIGHT], COUPLE MOTION VECTOR TO VISION VECTOR, MOVE FORWARD, STOP). The control routine proceeds by stages, first centering the object, then aligning the direction of motion to that vision direction, next moving forward in that direction, and finally stopping when adjacent to the object. The operations of the system take place over successive execution cycles or time-steps.

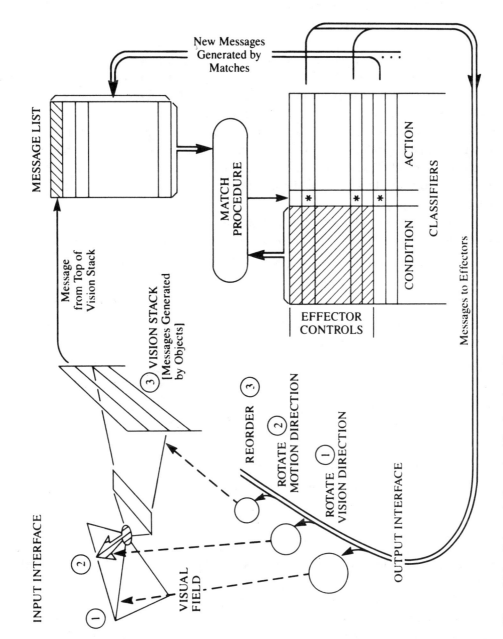

Figure 20-1: Schematic for a classifier-based cognitive system.

To define the classifier system, one first defines the input messages, then the condition parts of classifiers, and then the action parts of classifiers. Each of these is 16 bits long, though the present example is based on actual simulation in which they are 32 bits long.

The leftmost bit of a message is a tag, 1 for an input message and 0 for any other kind of message. The next 12 bits of an input message specify the properties of an object. (Note that these 12 bits can be used for entirely different purposes for messages with initial tag 0.) There are twelve independent properties, with 1 indicating the presence and 0 indicating the absence of a property in an object. For concreteness we will stipulate that the system is searching for objects—goal objects—that satisfy the condition #111000# ########. That is, it is searching for objects that have the first three properties and lack the next three, whether or not they have the remaining six properties.

The last 3 bits in an interface message give information about the relative position of the object in the field of vision. They are interpreted as follows:

bits 14, 15: 1,0 object left-of-center
0,1 object right-of-center
0,0 object centered

bit 16: 1 object adjacent
0 object not adjacent.

Thus, the message 11110001 01011100 indicates the presence in the visual field of a goal object that is left- of center and not adjacent, only the underlined bits being relevant to this interpretation.

Classifier *conditions* will be abbreviated as follows:

x = desired object x is present in the field of vision
c = object is centered
l = object is left-of-center
r = object is right-of-center
a = object is adjacent
$-a$ = object is not adjacent

Following these conventions, $[x,l,-a]$ specifies the condition 1111000# #####100, and so on.

The action part of each classifier specifies a 16-bit message issued when the conditions of the classifier are satisfied. Each such message will simply be abbreviated as the corresponding 16-bit integer. That is, "[4]" abbreviates the *message* 00000000 00000100, the tag 0 at the first position indicating that this is *not* an input message.

The classifier routine controls three effectors: an effector to move the direction of vision incrementally (15 degrees in the simulation) to the left or right, a second effector to set the direction of motion parallel to the direction of vision, and a third effector to cause the system to move forward one unit in the direction of motion. If no command is issued to a given effector during an execution cycle, that effector retains its last setting. In presenting the action effected by messages to effectors we will use

$L =$ rotate vision vector 15 degrees to the left
$R =$ rotate vision vector 15 degrees to the right
$P =$ set the move vector parallel to the vision vector
$G =$ move one unit forward in the move vector direction

There are nine classifiers in this illustrative system. The first four lead to operations by the remaining five, the next three cause output actions, the eighth causes the system to halt, and the ninth will be explained shortly.

$C1$ $[x,1]/[4]$
$C2$ $[x,r]/[5]$
$C3$ $[x,c,-a]/[6]$
$C4$ $[x,c,a]/[7]$
$C5$ $[4]/[8]$ [8] causes effector action L
$C6$ $[5]/[9]$ [9] causes effector action R
$C7$ $[6]/[10]$ [10] causes effector actions P and G
$C8$ $[7]/[11]$ [11] causes the cycling to halt
$C9$ $[4or5or6or7]/[0]$
(Note that the condition [4or5or6or7] is specified by the string 00000000 000001##.)

If an object of the desired type x appears at the far left of the field of vision at execution cycle t, classifier $C1$ is activated, placing message [4] on the message list at cycle $t + 1$. Assuming the object x is still left-of-center, the classifiers $C1$, $C5$, and $C9$ become active at cycle $t + 1$ and the message list consists of 4 messages: [4], [8], [0], and the message from the input interface. This list of messages continues until x is centered as a result of the repetitions of the L command, whereupon $C3$ would be activated, and so on (see table 20-1).

Note that message [4] provides a recording of the message from the input interface, coupling this information to the classifier $C5$ ($[4]/[8]$), which causes effector action L. Any message $[m]$ could have been used for this purpose; for example, the pair of classifiers $[x,1]/[m]$ and $[m]/[8]$ would have produced the same action L. It is this "internal" recoding that permits the classifier systems to carry out arbitrary computations, so that formally speaking classifier languages are computationally complete.

In detail, the execution sequence of the classifier system proceeds as shown in table 20-1. It is clear that the classifier [4or5or6or7]/[0] plays no role in this example. It is inserted to illustrate the concept of a *support* classifier, which is useful when the bucket-brigade algorithm (see section 20.5) is incorporated into this classifier

Table 20-1: Example of a typical execution sequence.

Major Cycle (Time)	Active Classifiers	Message List
t	$C1$	11110001 10000100 [4]
$t + 1$	$C1, C5, C9$	11110001 10000100 [4] [8] [0]
$t + 2$	$C1, C5, C9$	11110001 10000100 [4] [8] [0]
⋮		
($t + c$ is the time at which object x is first centered.)		
$t + c$	$C3, C9$	11110001 10000000 [6] [0]
$t + c + 1$	$C3, C7, C9$	11110001 10000000 [6] [10] [0]
⋮		
($t + a$ is the time at which the system is first adjacent to object x.)		
$t + a$	$C4, C9$	11110001 10000001 [7] [0]
$t + a + 1$	$C4, C8, C9$	11110001 10000001 [7] [11] [0]
(The system has now halted adjacent to object x.)		

system. In that case the classifier [4or5or6or7]/[0] serves to reinforce the whole set of classifiers. With further additions such a classifier can be used to call the whole routine when an object x appears.

20.4.5 Use of Classifiers to Define Complex Entities and Hierarchies

The introduction to this chapter made the point that the ultimate limitations on definition are no greater for the environment-oriented approach than for the language-oriented approach, that limit being set by distinguishability. Section 20.4.3 showed that clusters of coupled classifiers can be arranged to respond to any chosen subset of the set of possible messages. Because messages are the unifying element of classifier systems—providing internal communication as well as communication from the environment—this capability provides broad powers of definition. There is not room here for a detailed exposition, but the possibility of defining objects involving complex combinations of categories and relations—Winston's definition of an *arch* (1975) is a simple example—can at least be made plausible.

First, networklike interactions of coupled classifiers, through the use of tags and conditions of varying generality, have already been discussed (section 20.4.3). When the condition part of a rule is satisfied and it is coupled into such an array, it acts by pointing to other classifiers that are to have their condition parts tested in turn. That is, the outgoing message is tagged so that it is attended to by the classifiers to which the rule is to be coupled. This operation is quite analogous to passing a marker over a link in NETL (Fahlman, 1979) or to moving down one of the links in a linked list.

Because messages are involved, not just markers, a great deal of information can be carried from point to point in the network. For instance, the tag of a message can indicate its point of origin, and other bits carry information passed through or recoded (see section 20.4.2). Because of the parallelism of classifier systems, clusters of coactive rules can be used to define categories and objects (see section 20.4.3 and 20.4.4). The pointing technique can be extended to include relations, coupling some classifiers in a cluster to other related clusters. Finally, default hierarchies develop naturally under the bidding process discussed in section 20.5. Under the bidding process, when two classifiers are satisfied, say by the same message, the one with the more specific condition (fewer #'s) usually becomes active. As the induction procedures add new candidates to the system (see section 20.5), the "specialists" (fewer #'s) serve as exceptions to the "generalists" (more #'s) under the competition induced by the bidding process. A specialist may in turn serve as a default for a still more specific classifier, whence the developing default hierarchy arises.

The combination of the default hierarchy, so realized, with the clusters of coupled classifiers provides an effect much like Fahlman's virtual copy (1979). Environmental messages cause the activation of a cluster of classifiers that provides the "frame" and specifics wherein the system builds its responses to the situation. The tag on the outgoing message from a cluster can indicate the presence of some complex object, such as an *arch,* while the pass through bits (see section 20.4.2) carry incidental information (color, size, etc.) possibly relevant to further processing. The processing can include expectations (classifiers satisfied by messages from the virtual copy but not yet supported by messages from the environment) and plans (coupled sequences of classifiers wherein only the first element of the sequence is activated by messages from the environment).

The object of the next section is to show how such structures can emerge, in response to experience, under the impetus of competition and learning and induction rules. Some early uses of classifier systems for realistic problems (Wilson, 1982; Goldberg, 1983) show that default hierarchies do emerge and that sequences of coupled classifiers sensitive to stage-setting situations do develop.

20.5 LEARNING AND INDUCTION

The essence of classifier systems is a parallelism and a standardization that permit both a "building block" approach to the processing of information and the use of competition to resolve conflicts. It is the latter property, competition, that makes possible an approach to learning that is both general and powerful.

Two kinds of learning algorithms are required if a classifier system is to adapt to changes in the domains and goals presented to it. The first is an algorithm that reinforces or apportions credit to rules already available to the system. (Samuel's 1959 paper is full of insights concerning this problem.) The second is an algorithm for generating new, plausible rules when the rules available prove inadequate. (Samuel calls this "the parameter problem," and it is the one problem on which he did not really make progress. Recently both Lenat [1983] and Hofstadter [1983] have offered interesting approaches to it.) Here, in order to exploit competition between classifiers, two new kinds of algorithm are introduced. The first, the apportionment-of-credit algorithm, is called a *bucket-brigade algorithm.* The second, the rule generation algorithm, is called a *genetic algorithm.*

20.5.1 Bucket-Brigade Algorithms

The bucket-brigade algorithm is designed to assign credit to each classifier in the system according to its overall usefulness in attaining system goals. To this end, each classifier in the system is assigned a value, called its *strength,* and it is this value that the bucket-brigade algorithm adjusts. The problem is easy enough when a classifier participates directly in goal-achieving action that produces payoff, but it is quite difficult to decide which of the classifiers active early in a sequence sets the stage for later successful actions. (In Samuel's terms, it is easy enough to credit classifiers that combine to produce a triple jump at some point in the game; it is much harder to decide which classifiers active earlier were responsible for changes that made the later jump possible.) By a combination of analysis, and simulation (Wilson, 1982; Goldberg, 1983), we can show that the bucket-brigade algorithm actually accomplishes this task.

The algorithm works, via a modification of the basic execution cycle, by introducing a competition between classifiers. Recall that, during the execution cycle, each classifier scans all the messages on the global message list, producing a new message from each message satisfying its conditions. That procedure is now modified so that satisfied classifiers must compete to get their messages on the message list. Each satisfied classifier makes a *bid* based on its strength, and only the highest bidding classifiers get their messages on the list. The size of the bid depends not only on the classifier's strength but also on its specificity. (Recall that the specificity of a classifier is measured by the number of non-#'s in its condition part.) Specifically, the bid produced by a classifier is proportional to the product of its strength ("past usefulness") and its specificity ("relevance"—the amount of information about the current situation incorporated in its condition part).

Formally, when the condition part of a classifier C is satisfied, it makes a bid

$$\text{Bid}(C,t) = cR(C)\text{Strength}(C,t)$$

where $R(C)$ is the specificity, equal to the number of non-#'s in the condition part of C divided by the length thereof; $S(C,t)$ is the strength of C at time t, and c is a constant considerably less than 1 (e.g., 1/8 or 1/16).

The *winning* (high) bidders place their messages on the message list and have their strength *reduced* by the amount of the bid (they are paying for the privilege of posting a new message):

$$\text{Strength}(C,t + 1) = \text{Strength}(C,t) - B(C,t)$$

for a winning classifier C. The classifiers $\{C'\}$ that sent the messages matched by this winner have their strengths *increased* by the amount of the bid (it is shared among them in the simplest version):

$$\text{Strength}(C',t + 1) = \text{Strength}(C',t) + a\text{Bid}(C,t)$$

where $a = 1/(\text{number of members of } \{C'\})$. (The senders are rewarded for setting up a situation usable by C.)

The bucket-brigade algorithm treats each classifier as a kind of middleman in a complex economy, the strength of a classifier measuring its ability to turn a "profit." As a middleman, the classifier only deals with its suppliers—the classifiers that send messages satisfying its conditions—and its consumers—the classifiers that are in turn satisfied by the messages it sends. Whenever a classifier wins a bidding competition, it initiates a transaction in which it pays out part of its strength to its suppliers and then receives similar payments from its consumers.

The classifier's strength is a kind of capital. If a classifier receives more from its consumers than it paid out, it has made a profit, that is, its strength is increased. This is likely to occur only if the consumer in turn is profitable. This chain leads to the ultimate consumers, the classifiers that attain goals directly and receive payoff directly from the environment. That is, certain actions are immediately rewarded or reinforced by the environment; this payoff for goal attainment is added to the strengths of all classifiers active at that time. The profitability of other classifiers depends upon their being coupled into sequences leading to payoff. Thus, the bucket-brigade assures that early-acting, stage-setting classifiers receive credit if they (on average) make possible later, overtly rewarding acts.

It is worth noting that some of the fixed-point theorems of mathematical economics provide a way of proving the above for environments that have "stable" statistics.

20.5.2 Genetic Algorithms

Once strengths can be assigned to classifiers, a basis exists for generating new classifiers to enter the competition. In broadest terms the genetic algorithm uses high-strength classifiers as progenitors for new classifiers to be tested under the bucket brigade. Because of the parallelism of classifier systems, newly generated classifiers can be inserted into the "population" without the system's repertoire in well-practiced situations being seriously disrupted (see below). It is vital to the understanding of genetic algorithms to know that even the simplest versions act much more subtly than "random search with preservation of the best" (contrary to common misreading of genetics as a process primarily driven by mutation). Genetic algorithms have been studied intensively through analysis (Holland, 1975; Bethke, 1980) and simulation (DeJong, 1980; Smith, 1980; Booker, 1982; and others).

Although genetic algorithms act subtly, the basic execution cycle (the "central loop") is quite simple:

1. Select pairs from the set of classifiers according to strength—the stronger the classifier, the more likely its selection.
2. Apply genetic operators to the pairs, creating "offspring." Chief among the genetic operators is crossover, which simply exchanges a randomly selected segment between the pairs (see figure 20-3).
3. Replace the weakest classifiers with the offspring.

The effect of this procedure is to emphasize various combinations of defining elements—schemata—as building blocks for the construction of new classifiers. The tentative nature of the classifiers constructed in this way is pointed up by step 3 above. They will be displaced if they do not acquire strength under the bucket-brigade algorithm. Note that a newly constructed classifier gains or loses strength (aside from certain "taxations") only when its condition is satisfied and it wins the bidding competition to become active. As will be seen, this has much to do with the overall system's gracefulness relative to the insertion of new rules.

20.5.2.1 Definitions

To begin, let us consider the set C of all strings of length k over an alphabet of n letters. For example, the alphabet could be $\{1,0,\#\}$ so that the strings designate condition parts or message parts for classifiers. In the standard terminology of genetics these strings would be called *genotypes* and the values for individual letters in a string would be called *alleles*. The *set* of strings being tested at a given time (e.g., a classifier system) is called a *population*. In brief, and very roughly, a genetic algorithm can be looked upon as a sampling procedure that draws samples from the set **C**; each sample drawn has a value, the *fitness* of the corresponding genotype. From this viewpoint, the classifier system at time *t*—call it $B(t)$—is a set of classifiers drawn from **C**, and the fitness of each classifier is its strength. The genetic algorithm uses the fitnesses of the genotypes in $B(t)$ to generate new genotypes for test.

As will soon be seen in detail, the genetic algorithm uses the familiar "reproduction according to fitness" in combination with certain genetic operators (e.g., crossover; see below) to generate the new genotypes (classifiers). This process progressively biases the sampling procedure toward the use of *combinations* of alleles (building blocks) associated with above-average fitness. Surprisingly, in a population of size *M*, the algorithm effectively exploits some multiple of M^3 combinations in exploring **C**. (How this happens will be seen in a moment.) For populations of more than a few individuals this number, M^3, is vastly greater than the total number of alleles in the population. The corresponding speedup in the rate of searching **C**, a property called *implicit parallelism*, makes possible very high rates of adaptation. Moreover, because a genetic algorithm uses a distributed database (the population) to generate new samples, it is all but immune to some of the difficulties—false peaks, discontinuities, high-dimensionality, and so on—that commonly attend complex problems.

The task now is to give some substance—and intuition—to this outline. An understanding of some of the advantages and limitations of genetic algorithms can be reached via three short steps. First, in order to describe the nonuniform sampling procedure generated by a genetic algorithm, a special class of subsets of **C** is defined. Then, in the second step, an explicit sampling procedure emphasizing the sampling of combinations is used to examine the role of these special subsets in the nonuniform sampling procedure. The final step is to show how the genetic algorithm accomplishes implicitly and rapidly what is an intolerable computational burden for the explicit procedure.

For the first step, the subsets (combinations) of interest, called *schemata*, can be characterized as follows: Much as in the definition of conditions for classifiers (see section 20.4.2), values are first fixed at a selected set of positions in the *k*-position strings. Note that for classifiers the strings are over the alphabet $\{1,0,\#\}$ rather than the alphabet $\{1,0\}$. By using a (new) "don't care" symbol * for positions not fixed, one can specify schemata quite compactly. Thus *0**#** . . . ** is the set of *all* conditions (or actions) having a 0 at position 2 and a # at position 5. The set of schemata is the set of all collections that can be defined in this way. Note that schemata for classifiers define subsets of the *space of possible conditions* (or actions), in contrast to the conditions themselves, which define subsets of the *space of messages*. Thus a schema constitutes a building block from which one can construct classifiers.

Parenthetically, schemata can also be characterized in a way familiar to mathematicians: If we look upon the k-position strings as vectors in a k-dimensional space (each component having one of n values $0, 1, \ldots, n - 1$), then the schemata are hyperplanes of the k-dimensional space. Schemata name particular subsets of the set $\mathbf{C}$ of k-position strings. These subsets are of interest because they correspond to particular combinations of letters and because they are easily and compactly defined by strings on an $n + 1$-letter alphabet $\{0, 1, \ldots, n - 1, *\}$.

(For simplicity, $n = 2$, implying binary strings, will be used throughout the rest of this subsection. For theoretical reasons it is usually advantageous to recode strings over large alphabets, $n > 2$, into binary strings. To apply the discussion directly to classifiers, simply increase n to 3, using the particular alphabet $\{1,0,\#\}$.)

Now it is time for the second step. For a better illustration of the way in which schemata can aid a search, an algorithm will be considered that manipulates schemata explicitly. Although this algorithm is an aid to understanding, it is impractical from the computational point of view because of the enormous amounts of time and storage it would require. The genetic algorithm, to be described in the third step accomplishes the same actions concisely and rapidly via an implicit manipulation. The explicit version involves the following steps:

1. Set $t = 0$ and generate, at random, a set $B(t)$ of M strings.
2. Observe the value of $v(C)$, the "fitness," of each string C in $B(t)$.
   (From a more formal point of view, steps 1 and 2 amount to sampling the random variable v, using a sample of size M taken from $\mathbf{C}$.)
3. Let $M(\mathbf{s}, t)$ be the number of strings in $B(t)$ belonging to the schema $\mathbf{s}$ (i.e., the strings are instances of $\mathbf{s}$). If $M(\mathbf{s}, t) > 0$ for $\mathbf{s}$, calculate the average value $\hat{v}(\mathbf{s}, t)$ of the strings in $B(t)$ belonging to that schema. Calculate, also, the average value $\hat{v}(t)$ of the set of M samples.
   (There will be somewhere between 2^k and $M*2^k$ schemata with one or more instances in $B(t)$. More formally, $\hat{v}(\mathbf{s}, t)$ is the marginal sample average of v over the subset $\mathbf{s}$.)
4. Select a new set $B(t + 1)$ of M strings so that the number of instances of each schema s in the new set is equal to

$$M(\mathbf{s}, t + 1) = [\hat{v}(\mathbf{s}, t)/\hat{v}(t)]*M(\mathbf{s}, t)$$

for as many schemata as possible.
   (Informally, this recursion says that schemata observed to be above average, $\hat{v}(\mathbf{s}, t) > \hat{v}(t)$, receive more samples on the next time-step. Similarly, below-average schemata receive fewer samples. At first sight it may seem impossible to meet this requirement in any meaningful way because there are so many schemata, but see below.)
5. Set t to $t + 1$ and return to step 2.

It is difficult to satisfy the requirement of step 4 because the schemata (hyperplanes) intersect each other over and over again. In fact there are so many intersections that *each* string belongs to 2^k distinct schemata. Thus any sample allocated to one schema is as well a sample of $2^k - 1$ other schemata. However, a little thought and some calculation show that it *is* possible to distribute M new samples so that all schemata *with more than a few elements* receive the requisite number of samples. (Note that this means that schemata with more than a few *'s in their defining strings can be sampled according to the dictates of step 4.) Actually to carry out the distribution explicitly, allocating samples schema by schema so that step 4 is satisfied, would require an enormous amount of computation.

Setting aside the difficulties of implementation, we find that the algorithm uses very plausible inferences in generating "fit" strings. Most importantly, it samples with increasing intensity schemata that contain strings of above-average strength. The net effect of increasing the proportion of samples allocated to above-average schemata is to move the overall average $\hat{v}(t)$ upward. Because the average $\hat{v}(t)$ increases with time, this sampling procedure is a global "force" driving the search into subsets observed to contain valuable strings. Moreover, because the algorithm works from a database of M points distributed over **C**, it is not easily caught on "false peaks" (local optima). (Standard optimization procedures work well only with single-peak functions, relying on a uniform random search for "starting points" when there are multiple peaks.) Overall, this algorithm is much more globally oriented than standard optimization procedures, searching through a great many schemata for regularities and interactions that can be exploited. This point has been established, for the algorithm described next, by extensive experimental comparisons between that algorithm and standard procedures (Bethke, 1980; DeJong, 1980).

Figure 20-2 illustrates the use of schemata to locate the global optimum of a function $v(x)$ on the interval [0,1]. The arguments of the function are represented as binary fractions so that, for example, the argument $x = 1/2$ is represented as 0.100 . . . 0. If we look upon the binary representations as strings, then the schema 1** . . . * is the subset of all arguments greater than or equal to 1/2, that is, the interval [1/2,1]. Similarly, the schema **1* . . . * is a set of intervals (see top half of figure 20-2) corresponding to all the binary fractions that have a 1 in the third place. Other schemata are determined accordingly. Regularities of the function, such as periodicities, trends, and so on, are readily exploited by the biasing of samples toward appropriate schemata. The genetic algorithm automatically takes advantage of such schemata, as will be seen in a moment.

From an intuitive point of view, good schemata (schemata containing strings of above-average fitness) can be thought of as useful building blocks for constructing new strings. For example, if the schemata 1*0** . . . ** and ***001** . . . ** are both good, then it seems reasonable to investigate strings constructed with these building blocks, namely, strings belonging to the schema 1*0001** . . . **. The power of this

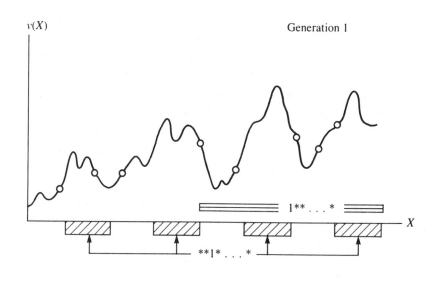

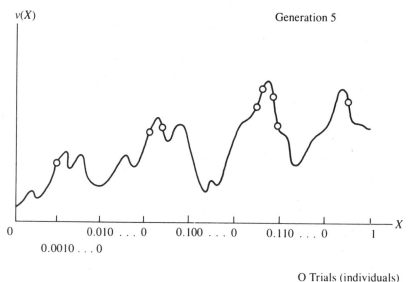

Figure 20-2: Example of function optimization by genetic algorithm.

kind of algorithm lies in its rapid accumulation of large numbers of better-than-average building blocks—building blocks that exploit regularities and interactions in the sample space **C**. By carefully choosing TM samples over T iterations, the algorithm accumulates information about a large number of potential building blocks, a number somewhere between 2^k and $TM2^k$.

Our objective now is to see how we can obtain the effects of this direct algorithm without paying the tremendous computational costs. This third step of the explanation involves, first, a specification of the genetic algorithm and, second, an explanation of its implicit manipulation of schemata (see figure 20-3).

The specification is as follows:

1. Set $t = 0$ and generate, at random, a set $B(t)$ of M strings.
2. Observe the value $v(C)$ of each string C in $B(t)$.
3. Compute the average strength $\hat{v}$ of the M strings in the database $B(t)$ and assign a normalized value $v(C)/\hat{v}$ to each string C in $B(t)$.
4. Assign each string in $B(t)$ a probability proportional to its normalized value and then select n, $n << M$, pairs of strings from $B(t)$ using this probability distribution.
5. Apply genetic operators to each pair, forming $2n$ new strings. The most important of the genetic operators is crossover (see figure 20-3): A position along the

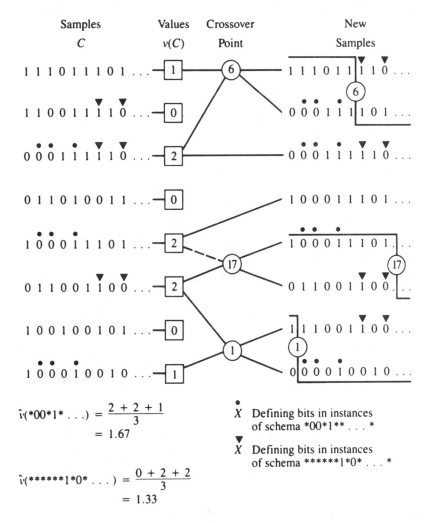

$$\hat{v}(*00*1* \ldots) = \frac{2 + 2 + 1}{3}$$
$$= 1.67$$

$$\hat{v}(******1*0* \ldots) = \frac{0 + 2 + 2}{3}$$
$$= 1.33$$

• $\overset{\bullet}{X}$ Defining bits in instances of schema *00*1** . . . *

▼ $\overset{▼}{X}$ Defining bits in instances of schema ******1*0* . . . *

Figure 20-3: Example of the genetic algorithm's effect on schemata.

string is selected at random, and then, in the pair being operated upon, the segments to the left of this position are exchanged. This simple operation has subtle effects when used in combination with the "emphasis" provided by step 3 as will be seen shortly. The other operators, such as *mutation* and *inversion*, have lesser roles in this use of the algorithm, mainly providing "insurance" against overemphasis of a given kind of schema. (See Holland, 1975, chap. 6, secs. 2, 3, and 4, for details.)

6. Select $2n$ strings from $B(t)$ and replace them with the $2n$ new strings resulting from step 4. (There are some technical issues involved in the selection of the strings to be replaced. These issues primarily concern limitations on the portion of the database allocated to strings of a given type. In effect each string belongs to a niche in the database and its spread is to be limited to the size—i.e., carrying capacity—of that niche. See Bethke, 1980, and DeJong, 1980, for details.)

7. Set t to $t + 1$ and return to step 2.

Unlike the earlier direct algorithm, the genetic algorithm never deals directly with schemata—it only manipulates the strings in $B(t)$. If one wishes to explore the action of the algorithm relative to schemata, it is helpful to divide the algorithm's action into two phases: Phase 1 consists of steps 2–4; phase 2 consists of steps 5–6.

Consider first what would happen if phase 1 were iterated without the execution of phase 2 (but with the replacement of strings in $B(t)$). In particular, let phase 1 be iterated $M/2n$ times (assuming for convenience that M is a multiple of $2n$). It is not difficult to show that the expected number of instances of a schema **s** at the end of this iteration is just $\hat{v}(\mathbf{s})$ times the number of instances at the outset (see Holland, 1975). This is true of *every* schema with instances in B, and this is just what was required of the direct algorithm in step 4.

What, then, is accomplished by phase 2? The problem is that phase 1 introduces no *new* strings into B; it merely introduces additional copies of strings already there. Phase 1 provides emphasis, but no new trials. The genetic operators, applied in phase 2, obviously modify the strings in B. It is a fundamental property of genetic algorithms (Theorem 6.2.3, Holland, 1975) that the emphasis provided by phase 1 is little disturbed by phase 2. That is, after phase 2, schemata with instances in B will largely have the *number* of instances provided by phase 1 *but they will be new instances.*

Thus the genetic algorithm as a whole generates new samples of *schemata* already present, increasing or decreasing the sampling rate according to the multiplier $\hat{v}(\mathbf{s},t)/\hat{v}(t)$, as desired. From the point of view of sampling theory, these new samples increase confidence in the estimates $\hat{v}(\mathbf{s})$ for each above-average schema **s** in B. Some calculation (Holland, 1975, chap. 4) shows that considerably more than M^3 schemata are so treated every $M/2n$ time-steps. Moreover, samples are generated for schemata not previously tried without this procedure being disrupted. All of this comes about through simple—and fast—manipulations of $2n$ strings per step. This implicit manipulation of a great many schemata via operations on relatively few strings is called *implicit parallelism.*

20.5.2.2 Application to Classifiers

How does all this apply to the generation of new classifiers? As mentioned, the strengths assigned by the bucket-brigade algorithm serve as the fitnesses of the classifiers. Because the parts of the classifier are strings of standard length k over a fixed alphabet $\{1,0,\#\}$, three possible alleles per locus, the procedures of the genetic algorithm are directly applicable. A combination of alleles that occurs in several strong classifiers—for example, a particular tag, or part of a message, or a combination of properties—automatically becomes a building block for the construction of new classifiers. Such combinations amount to schemata that are subject to the theorems concerning implicit parallelism.

If the classifier system is using M classifiers, it can be shown that, as the genetic algorithm generates new classifiers, it is effectively selecting amongst more than M^3 building blocks, each rated on the basis of past experience! The building blocks so manipulated determine important properties, such as classifier coupling and control sequencing (see section 20.4.3 and 20.4.4). Thus the genetic algorithm can encourage variants of useful subroutines, and it can generate hierarchical substructures for testing. In sum, the genetic algorithm offers an inductive procedure that is (1) fast (because of the implicit parallelism), (2) relatively immune to misdirection (because of the distributed database provided by the population), and (3) capable of sophisticated transfer of knowledge from one situation to another (because of the role of schemata).

It is important to note that, in general, the candidate rules generated by the genetic algorithm do *not* displace the parent rules. The parent rules simply supply copies of their parts for use by the genetic operators (such as crossover); they remain in the system in their original form. The offspring rules typically displace rules of low strength, thus eliminating rules that have not proved valuable to the system. As a consequence the parent rules, because of their high strength, will tend to remain in control of situations in which they acquired their strength. New rules typically get their chance in situations where none of the high-strength rules have their conditions satisfied. That is, they tend to fill new niches corresponding to domains in which the system has inadequate sets of rules. (This feature goes hand in hand with Scott's (1983) use of "play" as a means of reducing uncertainty about the environment.)

Ultimately, of course, new rules may outcompete their parents (or other relatives) if they prove superior under the bucket-brigade algorithm. The *explicit* parallelism, under which a variety of rules is active simultaneously, encourages the competition. The result is a system that can explore without disturbing well-established capabilities. In short, the system is graceful rather than brittle.

20.6 TESTS AND PROSPECTS

Several years ago a series of tests of simplified classifier systems (Holland and Reitman, 1978) demonstrated simple transfer of learning from problem to problem and showed that the genetic algorithm yielded learning, in that context, an order of magnitude faster than weight-changing techniques alone. The results were encouraging enough to spark a variety of subsequent tests at several places. Smith (then at the University of Pittsburgh, now at Carnegie-Mellon University) completed a classifier system (1980) that competed against Waterman's poker player (Waterman and Hayes-Roth, 1978)—also a learning program—with overwhelming success. Wilson (then at Polaroid, now at the Rowland Institute) used a classifier system (1982) with a genetic algorithm in a series of experiments involving TV-camera–mechanical-arm coordination, culminating in a successful demonstration of the segregation of the classifiers, under learning, into sets (Wilson calls them *demes*) corresponding to control subroutines. Booker has done an in-depth simulation study (1982) of classifier systems as cognitive models, with particular emphasis on the generation of cognitive maps under experience. More recently, Goldberg (1983) has demonstrated emergence of a default hierarchy in a study of the use of classifiers, under the genetic algorithm, as adaptive controls for gas pipeline transmission. There are several ongoing projects, including one that uses a classifier system to deal with the classification problem in KL-ONE (Forrest, 1982).

The more advanced properties of classifier systems are being tested with the help of a program, CS1, that is both a "compiler," allowing design and simulation of classifier systems on a serial computer, and a "test-bed," providing the means of simulating a wide range of environments for testing the learning algorithms. The current version provides the following facilities:

1. Simulation of a task environment consisting of up to 256 objects, each with up to thirty-two distinct features, emplaced on a 65,000-by-65,000 grid. Any or all of the objects may be mobile.

2. An input interface that consist of an arbitrarily shaped "vision cone" that views a local part of the surface (typically less than 1000 grid points) and uses feature detectors to generate an input message for each object in the vision cone.

3. An emulator for the classifier system that can retain, in random access memory, the description of over 1000 classifiers and a message list of up to thirty-two messages. This part of the system is written in machine language and can execute a basic time-step (all classifiers matched against all messages) in about 0.1 second. The overall system runs in close to real time, making it convenient to run long learning sequences in the simulated environment.

4. An output interface that permits manipulation of objects on the grid, movement over the grid, rotation of a visual cone, and in fact any other effector action conveniently specifiable by a subroutine.

5. Parameterized versions of both the bucket-brigade and genetic algorithms, including provisions for contingent activation of these algorithms (such as activation of the genetic algorithm when no classifier responds to an input message).

Studying full-fledged classifier systems is much like studying an ecology. There are niches, adaptations exploiting them, and shifting hierarchies of interaction—the emergence of parasitic classifiers has even been observed! Questions abound. Most pressing is the question of limitations. What is it that such systems *cannot* learn from experience? The author's observations to date indicate that general-purpose learning algorithms, given the right grist, can produce organizations that are detailed, appropriate, and subtle. This contradicts accepted wisdom in AI; somewhere there is a boundary (or set of them) that marks the limits of what can be accomplished reasonably with so-called weak methods. The author's impression is that the domain of such methods is *much* larger than is usually believed. Within this domain brittleness is no longer a bête noire.

Although most of the studies to date have dealt with systems that start with a tabula rasa—the most difficult test for a general-purpose learning procedure—this would not be the typical use of such systems. Classifier systems are general-purpose systems that can be programmed initially to implement whatever expert knowledge is available to the designers and their consultants. Learning then allows the system to expand, correct errors, and transfer information from one domain to another. In this context the question becomes one of how flexible—and graceful—such a system can be. It is important to provide ways of instructing such systems so that they can generate rules—hypotheses to be held tentatively—on the basis of advice. Little has been done in this direction.

Much more remains to be discovered about conditions that induce a classifier system to construct models of its environment for purposes of planning and look-ahead. It is particularly important to understand how look-ahead and virtual explorations can be incorporated without other activities of the system being disturbed. Ultimately the question is whether such systems can develop symbols (cf. Hofstadter, 1983) and use them, via abstract models, to generate plans and expectations.

ACKNOWLEDGMENT

This research was supported in part by the National Science Foundation under grants IST-8018043, MCS-7826016, and MCS-8305830.

References

Bethke, A. D., "Genetic Algorithms as Function Optimizers," Ph.D. diss., Department of Computer and Communication Sciences, University of Michigan, 1980.

Booker. L.. "Intelligent Behavior as an Adaptation to the Task Environment," Ph.D. diss.. Department of Computer and Communication Sciences, University of Michigan, 1982.

Davis. R.. and King. J.. "An Overview of Production Systems," in *Machine Intelligence 8,* E. W. Elcock, and D. Michie (Eds.), American Elsevier, New York, 1977.

DeJong. K. A.. "Adaptive System Design—A Genetic Approach," *IEEE Transactions: Systems, Man, and Cybernetics,* Vol. 10, No. 9, 1980.

Duda. R. O.. and Shortliffe. E. H., "Expert Systems Research," *Science,* Vol. 220, pp. 261–68, 1983.

Fahlman. S. E.. *NETL: A System for Representing and Using Real-World Knowledge,* MIT Press, Cambridge, 1979.

Forrest. S.. "A Parallel Algorithm for Classification of KL-ONE Networks," Consul Note No. 15, USC/ Information Sciences Institute, 1982.

Goldberg. D.. "Computer Aided Gas Pipeline Operation Using Genetic Algorithms and Rule Learning," Ph.D. diss.. Department of Civil Engineering, University of Michigan, 1983.

Hofstadter. D. R.. "Artificial Intelligence: Subcognition as Computation," in *The Study of Information,* F. Machlup and U. Mansfield (Eds.), Wiley, New York, 1983.

Holland. J. H., *Adaptation in Natural and Artificial Systems,* University of Michigan Press, Ann Arbor, 1975.

Holland. J. H., and Reitman, J. S., "Cognitive Systems Based on Adaptive Algorithms," in *Pattern-Directed Inference Systems,* D. A. Waterman and F. Hayes-Roth (Eds.), Academic Press, New York, 1978.

Lenat, D. B., "The Role of Heuristics in Learning by Discovery: Three Case Studies," in *Machine Learning: An Artificial Intelligence Approach,* R. S. Michalski, J. G. Carbonell, and T. M. Mitchell (Eds.), Tioga, Palo Alto, Calif., 1983.

McDermott, J., and Forgy, C., "Production System Conflict Resolution Strategies," in *Pattern-Directed Inference Systems,* D. A. Waterman, and F. Hayes-Roth (Eds.), Academic Press, New York, 1978.

Samuel, A. L., "Some Studies in Machine Learning Using the Game of Checkers," *IBM Journal of Research and Development,* Vol. 3, pp. 211–32, 1959.

Scott, P., "Knowledge-Oriented Learning," *Proceedings of the Eighth IJCAI,* Karlsruhe. W. Ger., pp. 432–35, 1983.

Smith, S., "A Learning System Based on Genetic Algorithms," Ph.D. diss.. Department of Computer Science, University of Pittsburgh, 1980.

Waterman, D. A., and Hayes-Roth, F. (Eds.), *Pattern-Directed Inference Systems,* Academic Press, New York, 1978.

Wilson, S., "Adaptive 'Cortical' Pattern Recognition," Internal Report, Research Laboratories, Polaroid Corporation, 1982.

Winston, P. H.. "Learning Structural Descriptions from Examples," in *The Psychology of Computer Vision,* P. H. Winston (Ed.), McGraw-Hill, New York, 1975.

Using Genetic Algorithms For Supervised Concept Learning

William M. Spears

Navy Center for Applied Research in AI

Naval Research Laboratory

Washington, D.C. 20375

SPEARS@AIC.NRL.NAVY.MIL

Kenneth A. De Jong

Computer Science Department

George Mason University

Fairfax, VA 20030

KDEJONG@AIC.GMU.EDU

Abstract

Genetic Algorithms (GAs) have traditionally been used for non-symbolic learning tasks. In this paper we consider the application of a GA to a symbolic learning task, supervised concept learning from examples. A GA concept learner (GABL) is implemented that learns a concept from a set of positive and negative examples. GABL is run in a batch-incremental mode to facilitate comparison with an incremental concept learner, ID5R. Preliminary results support that, despite minimal system bias, GABL is an effective concept learner and is quite competitive with ID5R as the target concept increases in complexity.

1. Introduction

There is a common misconception in the machine learning community that Genetic Algorithms (GAs) are primarily useful for non-symbolic learning tasks. This perception comes from the historically heavy use of GAs for complex parameter optimization problems. In the machine learning field there are many interesting parameter tuning problems to which GAs have been and can be applied, including threshold adjustment of decision rules and weight adjustment in neural networks. However, the focus of this paper is to illustrate that GAs are more general than this and can be effectively applied to more traditional symbolic learning tasks as well.†

To support this claim we have selected the well-studied task of supervised concept learning [Mitchell78, Michalski83, Quinlan86, Rendell89]. We show how concept learning tasks can be represented and solved by GAs, and we provide empirical results which illustrate the performance of GAs relative to a more traditional method. Finally, we discuss the advantages and disadvantages of this approach and describe future research activities.

---

† For an introduction to Genetic Algorithms, please see [Goldberg89].

2. Supervised Concept Learning Problems

Supervised concept learning involves inducing concept descriptions from a set of examples of a target concept (i.e., the concept to be learned). Concepts are represented as subsets of points in an n-dimensional feature space which is defined *a priori* and for which all the legal values of the features are known.

A concept learning program is presented with both a description of the feature space and a set of correctly classified examples of the concepts, and is expected to generate a reasonably accurate description of the (unknown) concepts. Since concepts can be arbitrarily complex subsets of a feature space, an important issue is the choice of the concept description language. The language must have sufficient expressive power to describe large subsets succinctly and yet be able to capture irregularities. The two language forms generally used are decision trees [Quinlan86] and rules [Michalski83].

Another important issue arises from the problem that there is a large (possibly infinite) set of concept descriptions which are consistent with any particular finite set of examples. This is generally resolved by introducing either explicitly or implicitly a bias (preference) for certain kinds of descriptions (e.g., shorter or less complex descriptions may be preferred).

Finally, there is the difficult issue of evaluating and comparing the performance of concept learning algorithms. The most widely used approach is a *batch mode* in which the set of examples is divided into a training set and a test set. The concept learner is required to produce a concept description from the training examples. The validity of the description produced is then measured by the percentage of correct classifications made by the system on the second (test) set of examples with no further learning.

The alternative evaluation approach is an *incremental mode* in which the concept learner is required to produce a concept description from the examples seen so far and to use that description to classify the next incoming example. In this mode learning never stops, and evaluation is in terms of learning curves which measure the predictive performance of the concept learner over time.

3. Genetic Algorithms and Concept Learning

In order to apply GAs to a particular problem, we need to select an internal representation of the space to be searched and define an external evaluation function which assigns utility to candidate solutions. Both components are critical to the successful application of the GAs to the problem of interest.

3.1. Representing the Search Space

The traditional internal representation used by GAs involves using fixed-length (generally binary) strings to represent points in the space to be searched. This representation maps well onto parameter optimization problems and there is considerable evidence (both theoretical and empirical) as to the effectiveness of using GAs to search such spaces [Holland75, DeJong85, Goldberg89, Spears90]. However, such representations do not appear well-suited for representing the space of concept descriptions which are generally symbolic in nature, which have both syntactic and semantic constraints, and which can be of widely varying length and complexity.

There are two general approaches one might take to resolve this issue. The first involves changing the fundamental GA operators (crossover and mutation) to work effectively with complex non-string objects [Rendell85]. This must be done carefully in order to preserve the properties which make the GAs effective adaptive search procedures (see [DeJong87] for a more detailed discussion). Alternatively, one can attempt to construct a string representation which minimizes any changes to the GAs without adopting such a convoluted representation as to render the fundamental GA operators useless.

We are interested in pursuing both approaches. Our ideas on the first approach will be discussed briefly at the end of the paper. In the following sections we will describe our results using the second approach.

3.2. Defining Fixed-length Classifier Rules

Our approach to choosing a representation which results in minimal changes to the standard GA operators involves carefully selecting the concept description language. A natural way to express complex concepts is as a disjunctive set of (possibly overlapping) classification rules (DNF). The left-hand side of each rule (disjunct) consists of a conjunction of one or more tests involving feature values. The right-hand side of a rule indicates the concept (classification) to be assigned to the examples which match its left-hand side. Collectively, a set of such rules can be thought of as representing the (unknown) concepts if the rules correctly classify the elements of the feature space.

If we allow arbitrarily complex terms in the conjunctive left-hand side of such rules, we will have a very powerful description language which will be difficult to represent as strings. However, by restricting the complexity of the elements of the conjunctions, we are able to use a string representation and standard GAs, with the only negative side effect that more rules may be required to express the concept. This is achieved by restricting each element of a conjunction to be a test of the form:

> return true if the value of feature i of the example is in the given value set, else return false.

For example, rules might take the following symbolic forms:

> if F1 = blue then it's a block

or

> if (F2 = large) and (F5 = tall or thin) then it's a widget

or

> if (F1 = red or white or blue) and (10 < F4 < 20) then it's a clown

Since the left-hand sides are conjunctive forms with internal disjunction, there is no loss of generality by requiring that there be *at most one test for each feature* (on the left hand side of a rule).

With these restrictions we can now construct a fixed-length internal representation for classifier rules. Each fixed-length rule will have N feature tests, one for each feature. Each feature test will be represented by a fixed length binary string, the length of which will depend of the type of feature (nominal, ordered, etc.).

For nominal features with k values we use k bits, 1 for each value. So, for example, if the legal values for F1 are the days of the week, then the pattern 0111110 would represent the test for F1 being a weekday.

Intervals for features taking on numeric ranges can also be encoded efficiently as fixed-length bit strings, the details of which can be seen in [Booker82]. For simplicity, the examples used in this paper will involve features with nominal values.

So, for example, the left-hand side of a rule for a 5 feature problem would be represented internally as:

F1	F2	F3	F4	F5
0110010	1111	01	111100	11111

Notice that a feature test involving all 1's matches any value of a feature and is equivalent to "dropping" that conjunctive term (i.e., the feature is irrelevant). So, in the above example only the values of F1, F3, and F4 are relevant. For completeness, we allow patterns of all 0's which match nothing. This means that any rule containing such a pattern will not match (cover) any points in the feature space. While rules of this form are of no use in the final concept description, they are quite useful as storage areas for GAs when evolving and testing sets of rules.

The right-hand side of a rule is simply the class (concept) to which the example belongs. This means that our "classifier system" is a "stimulus-response" system with no internal memory.

3.3. Evolving Sets of Classifier Rules

Since a concept description will consist of one or more classifier rules, we still need to specify how GAs will be used to evolve sets of rules. There are currently two basic strategies: the Michigan approach exemplified by Holland's classifier system [Holland86], and the Pittsburgh approach exemplified by Smith's LS-1 system [Smith83]. Systems using the Michigan approach maintain a population of *individual rules* which compete with each other for space and priority in the population. In contrast, systems using the Pittsburgh approach maintain a population of *variable-length rule sets* which compete with each other with respect to performance on the domain task.

Very little is currently known concerning the relative merits of the two approaches. As discussed in a later section, one of our goals is to use the domain of concept learning as a testbed for gaining more insight into the two approaches. In this paper we report on results obtained from using the Pittsburgh approach.† That is, each individual in the population is a variable length string representing an unordered set of fixed-length rules (disjuncts). The number of rules in a particular individual is unrestricted and can range from 1 to a very large number depending on evolutionary pressures.

Our goal was to achieve a representation that required minimal changes to the fundamental genetic operators. We feel we have achieved this with our variable-length string representation involving fixed-length rules. Crossover can occur anywhere (i.e., both on rule boundaries and within rules). The only requirement is that the corresponding crossover points on the two parents "match up semantically". That is, if one parent is being cut on a rule boundary, then the other parent must be also cut on a rule boundary. Similarly, if one parent is being cut at a point 5 bits to the right of a rule boundary, then the other parent must be cut in a similar spot (i.e., 5 bits to the right of some rule boundary).

The mutation operator is unaffected and performs the usual bit-level mutations.

3.4. Choosing a Payoff Function

In addition to selecting a good representation, it is important to define a good payoff function which rewards the right kinds of individuals. One of the nice features of using GAs for concept learning is that the payoff function is the natural place to centralize and make explicit any biases (preferences) for certain kinds of concept descriptions. It also makes it easy to study the effects of different biases by simply making changes to the payoff function.

For the experiments reported in this paper, we wanted to minimize any *a priori* bias we might have. So we selected a payoff function involving only classification performance (ignoring, for example, length and complexity biases). The payoff (fitness) of each individual rule set is computed by testing the rule set on the current set of examples and letting:

$$payoff\ (individual\ i) = (percent\ correct)^2$$

This provides a non-linear bias toward correctly classifying all the examples while providing differential reward for imperfect rule sets.

3.5. The GA Concept Learner

Given the representation and payoff function described above, a standard GA can be used to evolve concept descriptions in several ways. The simplest approach involves using a batch mode in which a fixed set of examples is presented, and the GA must search the space of variable-length strings described above for a set of rules which achieves a score of 100%. We will call this approach GABL (GA Batch concept Learner).

Due to the stochastic nature of GAs, a rule set with a perfect score (i.e., 100% correct) may not always be found in a fixed amount of time. So as not to introduce a strong bias, we use the following search termination criterion. The search terminates as soon as a 100% correct rule set is found within a user-specified upper bound on the number of generations. If a correct rule set is not found within the specified bounds or if the population loses diversity (> 70% convergence [De Jong75]), the GA simply returns the *best* rule set found. This incorrect (but often quite accurate) rule set is used to predict (classify) future examples.†

The simplest way to produce an incremental GA concept learner is to use GABL incrementally in the following way. The concept learner initially accepts a single example from a pool of examples. GABL is used to

---

Previous GA concept learners have used the Michigan approach. See [Wilson87] and [Booker89] for details.

In our experiments our upper bound was high enough that the GA always found a rule set with a perfect score. However, this slowed down running time dramatically.

create a 100% correct rule set for this example. This rule set is used to predict the classification of the next example. If the prediction is incorrect, GABL is invoked to evolve a new rule set using the two examples. If the prediction is correct, the example is simply stored with the previous example and the rule set remains unchanged. As each new additional instance is accepted, a prediction is made, and the GA is re-run in batch if the prediction is incorrect. We refer to this mode of operation as batch-incremental and we refer to the GA batch-incremental concept learner as GABIL.

4. Empirical Studies

4.1. Evaluating Concept Learning Programs

As suggested in the introduction, there are many ways to evaluate and compare concept learning programs: in either batch or incremental modes. We tend to favor incremental learning systems since the world in which most learning systems must perform is generally dynamic and changing. In this context we prefer the use of learning curves which measure the change in a system's performance over time in a (possibly) changing environment.

In the domain of supervised concept learning, this means that we are interested in situations in which examples are accepted one at a time. In this mode, a concept learner must use its current concept descriptions to classify the next example. The concept learner then compares its classification with the actual class of the example. Based on this comparison the concept learner may add that example to the existing set and attempt to reformulate new concept descriptions, or it may leave the current descriptions unchanged.

An incremental concept learner will make a prediction for each new instance seen. Each prediction is either correct or incorrect. We are interested in examining how an incremental system changes its predictive performance over time. Suppose each outcome (correct or incorrect) is stored. We could look at every outcome to compute performance, but this would only indicate the global performance of the learner (a typical batch mode statistic). Instead, we examine a small window of recent outcomes, counting the correct predictions within that window. Performance curves can then be generated which indicate whether a concept learner is getting any better at correctly classifying new (unseen) examples. The graphs used in the experiments in this paper depict this by plotting at each time step (after a new example arrives) the percent correct achieved over the last 10 arrivals (recent behavior).

4.2. Implementation Details

All of our experiments have been performed using a C implementation of the GAs. In all cases the population size has been held fixed at 100, the variable-length 2-point crossover operator has been applied at a 60% rate, the mutation rate is 0.1%, and selection is performed via Baker's SUS algorithm [Baker87].

4.3. Initial Experiments

The experiments described in this section are designed to demonstrate the predictive performance of GABIL as a function of incremental increases in the size and complexity of the target concept. We invented a 4 feature world in which each feature has 4 possible distinct values (i.e., there are 256 instances in this world). This means that rules map into 16-bit strings and the length of individual rule sets is a multiple of 16.

In addition to studying the behavior of our GA-based concept learner (GABIL) as a function of increasing complexity, we were also interested in comparing its performance with an existing algorithm. Utgoff's ID5R [Utgoff89], which is a well-known incremental concept learning algorithm, was chosen for comparison. ID5R uses decision trees as the description language and always produces a decision tree consistent with the instances seen.

We constructed a set of 12 concept learning problems, each consisting of a single target concept of increasing complexity. We varied the complexity by increasing both the number of rules (disjuncts) and the number of relevant features per rule (conjuncts) required to correctly describe the concepts. The number of disjuncts ranged from 1 to 4, while the number of conjuncts ranged from 1 to 3. Each target concept is labelled as nDmC, where n is the number of disjuncts and m is the number of conjuncts.

Each target concept is associated with one experiment. Within an experiment the number of disjuncts and conjuncts for the target concept remains fixed. The variation in target concept occurs between experiments. For each of the concepts, a set of 256 unique, noise free examples was generated *from the feature space* and labeled as positive or negative examples of the target concept. For the more complex concepts, this resulted in learning primarily from negative examples.

For each concept, the 256 examples were randomly shuffled and then presented sequentially as described above. This procedure was repeated 10 times for each concept and for each learning algorithm. The performance curves presented are the average behavior exhibited over 10 runs.†

ID5R and GABIL use significantly different approaches to concept learning. Therefore, we expect their performance behaviors to differ. As the number of

† It is not always possible for ID5R to make a prediction based on the decision tree. If it cannot use the tree to predict we let ID5R make a random prediction.

disjuncts and conjuncts increases, the target concept (viewed syntactically as a logical DNF expression) becomes more difficult. In general, a more complex target concept requires a larger decision tree (although this is not always true). ID5R relies upon Quinlan's information theoretic entropy measure to build its decision trees. This measure works well when individual features are meaningful in distinguishing an example as positive or negative. As the number of disjuncts and/or conjuncts increases, individual features become less informative, resulting in larger decision trees and poorer predictive performance. ID5R's information theoretic biases will therefore perform better on simpler target concepts.

GABIL, however, should perform uniformly well on target concepts of varying complexity. GABIL should not be affected by the number of conjuncts, since with our fixed-length rule representation, large conjunctions are no more difficult to find than small ones. There is also no bias towards a small number of disjuncts. Given these biases (and lack of biases), then, it is natural to expect that while ID5R will outperform GABIL on the simpler concepts, there will exist a frontier at which the situation will reverse.

For the sake of brevity we present graphs of 7 of the 12 experiments. Figure 1 depicts the comparative results on target concept 2D1C. It is representative of the results on all the 1 and 2 disjunct concepts. Figures 2 - 7 present the comparative results of applying both GABIL and ID5R to the more difficult concepts (3 and 4 disjuncts). Recall that each point on a curve represents the percent correct achieved over the previous 10 instances (and averaged over 10 runs). Note that this implies that the curves can only remain at 100% if the algorithms have learned the target concept by the 255th instance.

The graphs indicate that, on the simpler concepts, the predictive performance of ID5R improves more rapidly than that of GABIL. However, ID5R degrades in performance as the target concept becomes more

complex, and GABIL starts to win on the 4 disjunct concepts. We expect this trend to continue with even larger numbers of disjuncts and conjuncts.

Although it is natural to expect that a simple target concept (from a syntactic viewpoint) would have a small decision tree representation, this is only a rough generalization. We were surprised to see ID5R suffer the most on the 4D1C target concept, since syntactically the concept is only moderately complex. The target concept is of the form:

if (F1 = 0001) or (F2 = 0001) or (F3 = 0001)
or (F4 = 0001) then it's positive

This target concept is represented by ID5R as a decision tree of over 150 nodes. In fact, each negative example is represented by a unique leaf node in the decision tree. For this reason, ID5R cannot generalize over the negative examples, and has a good chance of predicting any negative example incorrectly. Furthermore, even the positive examples are not generalized well, resulting in prediction errors for positive examples. It is clear that the decision tree representation (which is also a bias) is poor for representing this particular concept. Target concept 4D1C represents a worst case, which explains why the difference between GABIL and ID5R is greatest for this concept. A similar situation occurs for target concepts 3D1C, 4D2C, and 4D3C, although to a lesser degree.

The experiments indicate that ID5R often degrades in performance as the number of disjuncts and conjuncts increases. ID5R's biases favor concepts that can be represented with small decision trees. The information theoretic measure favors those concepts in which individual features clearly distinguish target class membership. GABIL does not have these biases, and appears to be less sensitive to increasing numbers of disjuncts and conjuncts. GABIL does not degrade significantly with increasing target concept complexity and outperforms ID5R on 4 disjunct concepts. Since the syntactic complexity of a target concept corresponds roughly with the size of its decision tree representation, we expect this trend to continue with more difficult target concepts.

5. Further Analysis and Comparisons

We plan to perform additional experiments involving the comparison of GABIL with other concept learning programs such as Michalski's AQ15 [Michalski86], Quinlan's C4.5 [Quinlan89], and Clark's CN2 [Clark89] on artificial concepts as well as on some of the classical test sets such as the breast cancer data and the soybean plant disease data.

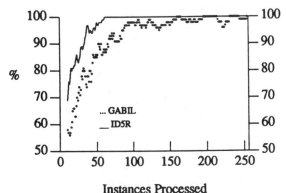

Fig 1. 2D1C

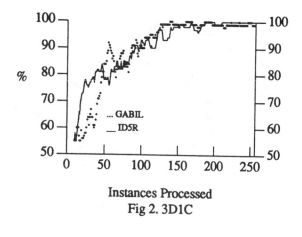

Instances Processed
Fig 2. 3D1C

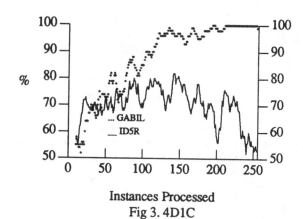

Instances Processed
Fig 3. 4D1C

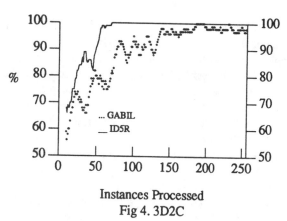

Instances Processed
Fig 4. 3D2C

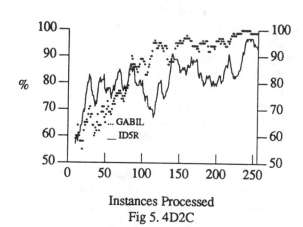

Instances Processed
Fig 5. 4D2C

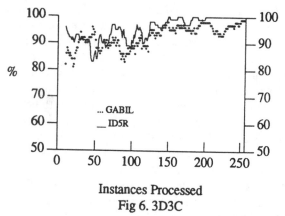

Instances Processed
Fig 6. 3D3C

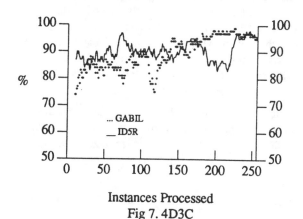

Instances Processed
Fig 7. 4D3C

We also plan to implement and analyze other GA-based concept learners. The first is a variation of the current one which is truly incremental rather than batch-incremental. We feel that this change will smooth out many of the bumps in the learning curves currently due to completely reinitializing the population when an incorrect classification is made on a new example.

We are also very interested in understanding the difference between using the Pittsburgh approach and the Michigan approach in this problem domain. The current fixed-length rule representation can be used directly in Michigan-style classifier systems. We plan to implement

such a system and compare the two approaches.

Finally, we noted early in the paper that there were two basic strategies for selecting a representation for the concept description language. In this paper we developed a representation which minimized the changes to standard GA implementations. We also plan to explore the alternative strategy of modifying the basic GA operators to deal effectively with non-string representations. In particular, we plan to use Michalski's VL1 language and compare this approach to using GAs with the current work.

6. Conclusions

This paper presents a series of initial results regarding the use of GAs for symbolic learning tasks. In particular, a GA-based concept learner is developed and analyzed. It is interesting to note that reasonable performance is achieved with minimal bias. There is no preference for shorter rule sets, unlike most other concept learning systems. The initial results support the view that GAs can be used as an effective concept learner although they may not outperform algorithms specifically designed for concept learning when simple concepts are involved.

This paper also sets the stage for additional comparisons between GAs and other concept learning algorithms. We feel that such comparisons are important and encourage the research community to develop additional results on these and other problems of interest.

Acknowledgements

We would like to thank Diana Gordon for her support and for many discussions on the biases in supervised concept learning systems. Diana was also instrumental in helping us design our experimental methodology. We would also like to thank John Grefenstette and Alan Schultz for many useful comments about GABIL and crossover.

References

Baker, James E. (1987). Reducing Bias and Inefficiency in the Selection Algorithm, *Proc. 2nd Int'l Conference on Genetic Algorithms and their Applications*, 14-21.

Booker, Lashon B. (1982). *Intelligent Behavior as an Adaptation to the Task Environment*, Doctoral Thesis, CCS Department, University of Michigan.

Booker, Lashon B. (1989). Triggered Rule Discovery in Classifier Systems, *Proc. 3rd Int'l Conference on Genetic Algorithms and their Applications.*

Clark, P. and Niblett, T. (1989). The CN2 Induction Algorithm. *Machine Learning*, Volume 3, Number 4.

De Jong, Kenneth A. (1975). *An Analysis of the Behavior of a Class of Genetic Adaptive Systems*, Doctoral thesis, Dept. Computer and Communication Sciences, University of Michigan, Ann Arbor.

De Jong, Kenneth A. (1985). Genetic Algorithms: a 10 Year Perspective, *Proc. 1st Int'l Conference on Genetic Algorithms and their Applications*, 169-177.

De Jong, Kenneth A.(1987). Using Genetic Algorithms to Search Program Spaces, *Proc. 2nd Int'l Conference on Genetic Algorithms and their Applications.*

Goldberg, David E. (1989). *Genetic Algorithms in Search, Optimization & Machine Learning*, Addison-Wesley Publishing Company, Inc.

Holland, John H. (1975). *Adaptation in Natural and Artificial Systems*, The University of Michigan Press.

Holland, John H. (1986). Escaping Brittleness: The Possibilities of General-Purpose Learning Algorithms Applied to Parallel Rule-Based Systems. In R. Michalski, J. Carbonell, and T. Mitchell (Eds.), *Machine Learning: An Artificial Intelligence Approach* (Vol. 2). Morgan Kaufmann Publishers, Los Altos, CA.

Mitchell, T. (1978). *Version Spaces: An Approach to Concept Learning*. Doctoral thesis, Stanford University, Stanford, CA.

Michalski, R. (1983). A Theory and Methodology of Inductive Learning. In R. Michalski, J. Carbonell, and T. Mitchell (Eds.), *Machine Learning: An Artificial Intelligence Approach* (Vol. 1). Tioga Publishing Co., Palo Alto, CA.

Michalski, R., Mozetic, I., Hong, J., and Lavrac, N. (1986). The AQ15 Inductive Learning System: An Overview and Experiments. University of Illinois Report Number UIUCDCS-R-86-1260.

Quinlan, J. R. (1986). Induction of Decision Trees. *Machine Learning*, Volume 1, Number 1.

Quinlan, J. R. (1989). Documentation and User's Guide for C4.5. (unpublished).

Rendell, L. (1985). Genetic Plans and the Probabilistic Learning System: Synthesis and Results. *Proc. 1st Int'l Conference on Genetic Algorithms and their Applications.*

Rendell, L., Cho, H., and Seshu, R. (1989). Improving the Design of Similarity-Based Rule-Learning Systems. *International Journal of Expert Systems*, Volume 2, Number 1.

Smith, S. F. (1983). Flexible Learning of Problem Solving Heuristics Through Adaptive Search, *Proc. 8th IJCAI*, August 1983.

Spears, W. M. (1990). *Using Neural Networks and Genetic Algorithms as Heuristics for NP-Complete Problems*, Masters thesis, CS Department, George Mason University.

Utgoff, Paul E. (1986). Shift of Bias for Inductive Concept Learning. In R. Michalski, J. Carbonell, and T. Mitchell (Eds.), *Machine Learning: An Artificial Intelligence Approach* (Vol. 2). Morgan Kaufmann Publishers, Los Altos, CA.

Utgoff, Paul E. (1989). Improved Training via Incremental Learning, *Proc. of the 6th Int'l Workshop on Machine Learning*, 62-65.

Wilson, S.W. (1987). Classifier Systems and the Animat Problem, *Machine Learning* Volume 2, Number 4.

SCHEMA SURVIVAL RATES AND HEURISTIC SEARCH
IN GENETIC ALGORITHMS

Bill P. Buckles, Frederick E. Petry, Rebecca L. Kuester

Department of Computer Science
Center for Intelligent and Knowledge-based Systems
Tulane University
New Orleans, Louisiana 70118

Keywords: genetic algorithms, traveling salesman problem, probabalistic search, crossover rules

Abstract

Genetic Algorithms are a relatively new paradigm for search in A.I. which are based on the principles of natural selection. They are probabilistic algorithms that are not yet well understood. It is shown here that for certain kinds of search problems, called permutation problems, the ordinary rule for intermixing the genes between two organisms leads to longer search chains than are necessary. A schema is a partially completed organism. Its order is the number of fixed components and its length is the distance between its first and last fixed component. A schema is compact if its length and order are nearly equal. The solution to many permutation problems such as the traveling salesman problem, consist of the concatenation of a series of compact schema. It is shown that the survival rate of compact schema is directly proportional to the quality of the solution after a fixed number of iterations. Yet the ordinary gene intermixing method, called a crossover rule, separates the parents of a new organism at almost the precise point at which the compact schema survival rate is at a minimum. A variation of the crossover rule is proposed that takes advantage of the knowledge of survival rates on the quality of the solution.

1. Introduction

Genetic algorithms (GAs) are a new A.I. paradigm that arose from the investigations of cellular automata in the 1970s. The formal theory was initially developed by John Holland [5] and his students and in recent years have been applied to problems as diverse as pattern recognition [1] and optimization [8]. GAs are probabilistic algorithms and their behavior is still in many ways not well understood. An excellent text is presently available describing most of their known properties [4]. The purpose of this study is to investigate and resolve their behavior with respect to the crossover operator for a specific kind of optimization problem for which the output consists of a permutation of the input.

The premier permutation problem is known as the traveling salesman problem. The objective is to find the tour of shortest length on an undirected graph that begins at any node, visits all nodes, and returns to the starting node. That is, given n points, $\{A, B, ...\}$, and permutations, $\sigma_1, \sigma_2, ..., \sigma_{n!}$, the objective is to choose σ_i such that the sum of the Euclidean distances between each node and its successor is minimized. The successor of the last node in the permutation is the first one. The traveling salesman problem has been investigated several times in the past using GAs [6,8]. GAs have been used on an experimental basis for path planning for space-based robots [2,3].

2. Genetic Algorithms

GAs borrow much of their terminology from natural genetics. An organism, for instance, is a string of values called alleles which are defined over some alphabet. Frequently, the alphabet used is the binary digits $\{0, 1\}$. Thus, a sample organism of length 8 would appear externally as 00101101. For a permutation problem, however, each organism must represent a sequence of the alphabet. The allele values used here are the letters $\{A, B, ...\}$ and a sample organism of length 8 is BCHEGADF. The example represents a tour that begins at point B then goes to point C and so on. The successor to F is B, the beginning of the tour.

Figure 1 depicts an overview of a simple GA. A population is a set of organisms. An initial population is randomly generated and successive populations, called generations, are derived by applying the selection, crossover and mutation operators to the previous generation. The selection operator chooses two members of the present generation to participate in the later operations - crossover and mutation. In diagram form, Figure 1 shows a current generation being acted upon by the three operators to produce the successive generation.

Note in the figure that there is an intervening action called fitness function evaluation that assigns to each organism a value, noted as f_i. f_i is a figure of merit that is computed using any domain knowledge that applies. In principle, this is the only point in the algorithm that domain knowledge is necessary. Organisms are chosen using the fitness value as a guide, organisms with higher fitness values being chosen more often. Selecting organisms based on fitness value is a major factor in the strength of GAs as search algorithms.

There are two popular approaches for implementing selection. The first, called roulette selection, is to assign a probability to each organism, i, computed as the proportion, F_i

0-8186-2935-5/92 $3.00 © 1990 IEEE

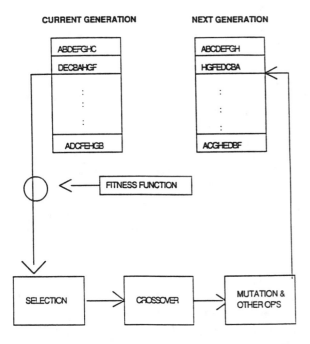

Figure 1. Principal Genetic Algorithm Components

$= f_i/\Sigma f_j$. A parent is then randomly selected based on this probability. A second method, called deterministic sampling, assigns to each organism, i, a value $C_i = RND(F_i \times popsize) + 1$ to each organism. (RND means round to integer and popsize means population size.) The selection operator then assures that each organism participates as a parent exactly C_i times.

A strategy called scaling is often used to bias the selection operator toward the more fit organisms even moreso. One method, linear scaling, determines for each generation the constants a and b and resets the fitness of organism i to $f_i = a f_i + b$ and F_i is computed with the revised fitness. The constants are chosen such that $f'_{avg} = a f_{avg} + b$, where f_{avg} is the mean fitness value. An option is to let $a = (m-1) f_{avg}/(f_{max}-f_{avg})$ and $b = f_{avg} (f_{max} - m f_{avg})/(f_{max}-f_{avg})$, where m is the number of offspring desired for the organism having the maximum fitness and f_{max} is the maximum fitness. If $f < 0$ for any organism then m must be lowered.

Selection raises the issue of fitness functions for the traveling salesman problem. A requirement of the above selection methods is that f_i be higher for organisms that represent better tours. However, better tours physically comprise lower Euclidean distances. Neither the longest nor shortest tour is known in advance. The method employed here was to first compute the Euclidean distance, D_i, for each organism then let $f_i = D_{max} - D_i$. Table 1 illustrates these fitness function concepts for an (unrealistically small) population of 5.

Crossover is the operator that intermixes the alleles of two parents to obtain an offspring. There exist many versions of crossover for problems over the binary alphabet but a more limited choice for permutation problems. There are three principal ones - order crossover, PMX crossover, and cycle crossover. There exist crossover methods designed specifically for shortest path problems[6], but the objective here is to investigate problem independent properties of permutation problems so these were not used. Appendix B contains a description of those crossover operators mentioned but not used in this study. Of the three principal ones, a previous study [7] indicated that order crossover is slightly more effective so it is the one used here.

Table 1. Illustration of Fitness Function Concepts

i	Organism	D_i	f_i	$\hat{f}_i$	F_i	C_i
1	BEFCAD	122	0	1.17	0.01	1
2	FEBACD	101	21	21.63	0.10	2
3	CDAFBE	80	42	42.09	0.19	2
4	DAFCBE	50	72	71.31	0.31	2
5	BDAEFC	30	92	90.80	0.40	3

Preparatory to applying order crossover, two random crosspoints are selected. Alleles from the first parent that fall between the two crosspoints are copied into the same positions of the offspring. The remaining allele order is determined by the second parent. Nonduplicative alleles are copied from the second parent to the offspring beginning at the position following the second crosspoint. Both the second parent and the offspring are traversed circularly from that point. A copy of the parent's next nonduplicative allele is placed in the next available child position. An example for which the random crosspoints are 3 and 6 follows.

Parent 1: ABC|GHB|DE

Parent 2: HDE|FGC|BA

Child: EFC|GHB|AD

Crossover need not be applied to obtain each offspring in the new generation. Often the best solution from the current generation is placed unaltered into the next generation. This is known as the elitist strategy.

The mutation operator offers the opportunity for new genetic material to be introduced into a population. From the theoretical perspective, it assures that, given any population, the entire search space is connected. The new genetic material does not originate from the parents and is not introduced into the child by crossover. Rather, it occurs a small percentage of the time after crossover. The mutation operator performs, as in nature, by randomly changing alleles. For a problem over the binary alphabet, the original allele is exchanged for its complement. In a permutation problem, arbitrarily changing a single allele value would not preserve allele uniqueness. The method frequently used for permutation problems is to interchange two randomly selected positions, thus preserving allele uniqueness.

There exist several stopping criteria for the algorithm. It may be halted when all organisms in a generation are identical, when $f_i = f_j$ for all i and j, or when $|f_i - f_j| < TOL$ for some small value TOL and all i and j. The stopping criterion used here is to halt after a fixed number of evaluations and take as the solution the best tour discovered thus far.

3. Parameter Analysis for Order Crossover

Given an organism of length n, there are n^2 ways to choose a segment cut. The probability that the length, K, of a cut is 1, $P[K=1]$, is $1/n$. For any other value

$$P[K=i] = 2[n-(i-1)/n^2]$$

In general the average value of K is

$$E(K) = 1/n + 2/n^2 \sum_{i=2}^{n} i\,(n-(i-1))$$

$$= n + 2 - 2/n^2 \sum_{i=1}^{n} i^2$$

$$= 1 + n/3 + 1/(3n) \qquad (1)$$

A schema for a permutation problem is of the form (a # # b c # # # # # #) where the symbol # represents "don't care". The order, o, of a schema is the count of non-# symbols. Its length, w, is the distance from the first to the last symbol. For the example, o = 3 and w = 5. For the traveling salesman problem, the schemas (a b # # # # # # #), (# # # a b # # # #), and (b # # # # # # # a) are the same due to the cyclic nature a tour. A schema for which o Iw is said to be compact and strictly compact if o = w. Note that the term "order" in order crossover has no connection with "order" as denoted by the symbol O. The former refers to sequence preservation and the latter to cardinality.

A population contains many schemas. The crossover and mutation operators act in conjunction with the selection operator to put "good" schemas called building blocks together into a single organism to form a good solution. Obviously, the good schemas for a traveling salesman problem are compact. Survival of good schemas is the objective of parametrically adjusting a GA. The problem of survival is discussed in [7] and extended here. Given K>w, a segment of length K contains K-w+1 schema as there are no end-around combinations. Thus, for parent 1 in order crossover, the probability of survival is the probability that the schema is within the cut.

$$P[\text{Sur} \mid \text{parent-1}] = (K-w+1)/\, n \qquad (2)$$

For survival of a schema in parent 2, o alleles must be present in positions corresponding to those in the schema and none of them may be within the cut of parent 1.

$$I[\text{Sur} \mid \text{parent-2}] \cong (1-K/n)^o \qquad (3)$$

The relation is approximately equal because the placement of the cut segment within the child separates the last allele taken from parent 2 from the first. The effect is negligible for large n and small w and is not taken into account in the formula. Note that for strictly compact schema, o and w are interchangeable in Equations (2) and (3).

Let $S_{o,i}$ be the set of strictly compact schemas of order o in parent i within an organism. For an organism of length n, $|S_{o,i}| = n$ since the length may extend from the right end back to the left end. Combining Equations 2 and 3, the expected value for the number of surviving schemas in an offspring is

$$M_n \cong |S_{o,1}|(K-w+1)/n + |S_{o,2}|(1-K/n)^w \qquad (4)$$

GAs are successful because they combine stability with enough perturbation to simultaneously maintain the good solutions while progressing toward better ones. Obvious hypotheses can be formulated concerning stability and perturbation and they can be expressed in terms of M. Is the best performance obtained when stability is given preference (survival rate is high) or when perturbation is given preference (survival rate is lower)? The experiments were designed to address these questions.

4. Experimental Results

Figure 2 shows a plot of M for n=16, n=30, and n=50. In the figure, it is assumed that o = w = 2. E(K) from Equation 1 is marked for each value of n. Note that it always occurs at or near the nadir of M. A new version of order crossover was developed that allowed control of the value of E(K). That is, once one end of a segment was identified randomly, the second endpoint was chosen (also randomly) such that after many trials the average crossover segment length would be a known fixed value.

To test each value of the controlled E(K), four tests were run, each starting with a different random number seed. Where a segment cut began near the end of an organism, it was allowed to "wrap-around". The result was taken as the average of the four runs. For the 16 city problem, each run consisted of 50 generations of 50(250 evaluations). Each run for the 30 city problem consisted of 500 generations each with a population of 100. That is, 50,000 tours were evaluated. For the 50 city problem, two independent series of tours were computed. In the first, 500 generations with populations of 100 were used (50,000 evaluations). In the second series, 1,000 generations of 100 were used (100,000 evaluations). The data for each problem is in the Appendix A. The mutation level was fixed at 10% for all runs. Selection was implemented using the roulette wheel method. Each population was scaled. An elitist strategy was employed.

Figures 3,4, and 5 show the result for n of 16, 30, and 50, respectively. The graphs consistently show that the performance is better for those regions in which M is high. On each graph the ordinary expected value of the length of a cut as obtained from Equation 1 is shown via a vertical line. The average of all tests is shown by the horizontal line.

5. Conclusions

Crossover operators specifically designed to solve the traveling salesman problem consistently achieve tours within 2-3% of the optimum with far fewer evaluations than used here [6]. The problem is based on compact schema, however, and the results given here show a weakness in the common permutation operators which are not based on domain knowledge. They do not maintain the correct balance between schema survival and the creation of new schema. The effect becomes more pronounced as the size of the problem grows due to a greater difference between the number of surviving schema in short or long cuts than in ones that approximate half the string length. It is recommended that future implementations of order crossover be modified to control the length of the average cut to be either short or long.

Our investigations did not include separation of initial search from the latter stages of optimization. It is entirely possible that mid-length cuts early, causing much perturbation, followed by controlled cuts later, emphasizing preservation, will further improve performance. This is an issue for further study.

Our less extensive testing of the PMX crossover operator showed the same trends. As noted, previous investigations [7] have indicated that for compact schemas the performance of order and PMX crossover closely approximate each other with order crossover being slightly better. An interesting future investigation would be the shortest path problem because the schema, while still compact, do not have the wrap-around characteristic.

References

[1] C.A. Ankenbrandt, B.P. Buckles and F.E. Petry, "Scene Recognition Using Genetic Algorithms with Semantic Nets", Pattern Recognition Letters, 11, pp 285-293, 1990.

[2] P. Baffes and L. Wang, "Mobile Transporter Path Planning", Proc. SOAR '89, Houston, TX, pp 51-59, July 1989.

[3] T. Cleghorn, P. Baffes and L. Wang, "Robot Path Planning Using a Genetic Algorithm",, Proc. SOAR '88, Houston, TX, pp 81-87, July 1988.

[4] D.E. Goldberg, Genetic Algorithms in Search, Optimization and Machine Learning, Addison-Wesley, Reading, MA, 1989.

[5] J.H. Holland, Adaptation in Natural and Artificial Systems, University of Michigan Press, Ann Arbor, 1975.

[6] P. Jog, J.Y. Suh and D.V. Gucht, "The Effects of Population Size, Heuristic Crossover and Local Improvement in a Genetic Algorithm for the Traveling Salesman Problem", Proc. Third Int. Conf. on Genetic Algorithms, Fairfax, VA, pp 110-115, June 1989.

[7] I.M. Oliver, D.J. Smith and J.R.C. Holland, "A Study of Permutation Crossover Operators on the Traveling Salesman Problem", Proc. Second Int. Conf. on Genetic Algorithms, Hillsdale, NJ, pp 224-230, June 1987.

[8] J.D. Schaffer, R.A. Caruana, L.J. Eshelman and R. Das, "A Study of Control Parameters Affecting Online Performance of Genetic Algorithms for Function Optimization", Proc. Third Int. Conf. on Genetic Algorithms, Fairfax, VA, pp 51-60, June 1989.

[9] D. Whitley, T. Starkweather and D. Fuquay, "Scheduling Problems and Traveling Salesman: The Genetic Edge Recommendation Operator", Proc. Third Int. Conf. on Genetic Algorithms, Fairfax, VA, pp 133-140, June 1989.

APPENDEX A

The coordinates for the three problems are given below.

The 16 city problem has an optimum tour of 232. The coordinates in order of the best solution are: (37,84), (41,94), (14,98), (2,99), (2,76), (25,62), (18,54), (4,50), (9,42), (13,40), (24,42), (36,38), (44,35), (54,62), (46,74).

The 30 city problem has an optimum tour of 421 according to [7]. The coordinates in order of the best solution are: (54,67), (54,62), (37,84), (41,94), (2,99), (7,64), (25,62), (22,60), (18,54), (4,50), (13,40), (18,40), (24,42), (25,38), (44,35), (41,26), (45,21), (58,35), (62,32), (82,7), (91,38), (83,46), (71,44), (64,60), (68,58), (83,69), (87,76), (74,78), (71,71), (58,69).

The 50 city problem has an optimum tour of 438. The coordinates in order of the best solution are: (41,94), (28,94), (14,98), (2,99), (4,86), (2,76), (7,64), (14,66), (25,62), (22,60), (18,54), (11,50), (4,50), (9,42), (13,40), (24,42), (25,38), (36,38), (44,35), (41,26), (45,21), (52,29), (58,35), (62,32), (70,24), (74,12), (82,7), (88,14), (92,24), (91,38), (88,44), (83,46), (71,44), (64,60), (68,58), (79,62), (83,69), (87,76), (80,80), (74,78), (71,71), (60,72), (58,69), (54,67), (54,62), 46,74), (40,76), (37,84), (40,88).

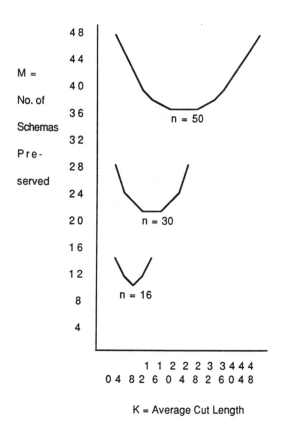

M =

No. of

Schemas

Pre-

served

n = 50

n = 30

n = 16

K = Average Cut Length

Figure 2. Plot of Average Cut Length vs.
Schema Survival Rate(o=w=2)

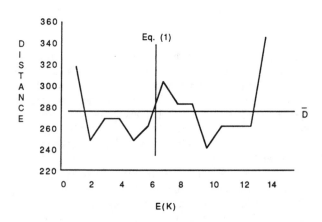

Eq. (1)

D̄

E(K)

Figure 3. Best tours for n = 16

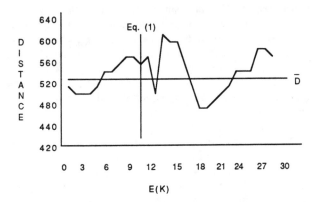

Eq. (1)

D̄

E(K)

Figure 4. Best tours for n = 30

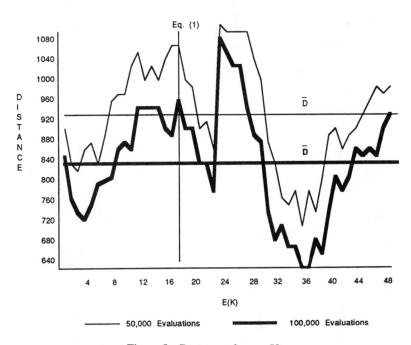

Eq. (1)

D̄

D̄

E(K)

50,000 Evaluations   100,000 Evaluations

Figure 5. Best tours for n = 50

APPENDEX B

Permutation crossover rules are those that operate under the conditions that each organism must be a permutation of the problem alphabet. Such rules are useful if the underlying problem is task scheduling or route planning. In the examples that follow, the problem alphabet is assumed to be {A, B, C, D, E, F, G, H}. Order crossover is discussed in the text. Others follow.

B.1 PMX Crossover

Initially, PMX (partially matched) crossover proceeds just as order crossover. Alleles from the first parent that fall between two randomly selected crossing sites are copied into the same positions of the offspring. The remaining allele positions are determined by the second parent during a two step process. First, alleles in the second parent not within the crossing sites are copied to the corresponding positions within the offspring. Next, each allele of the second parent within the crossing sites is placed in the offspring at the position occupied in the second parent by the allele from the first parent that displaced it. In the example below, A, H, and G displace in the offspring D, E, and F, respectively. D goes to position 1 which is the position with respect to the second parent that the displacing allele, A, occupies. E and F are placed in the positions by H and G, respectively.

    Parent 1:   FBC|AHG|DE

    Parent 2:   ABC|DEF|GH

    Child: DBC|AHG|FE

B.2 Cycle Crossover

Cycle crossover does not use crossing sites. A cycle is defined in a manner similar to an algebraic permutation group. To illustrate using the example below, compare the strings of parent 1 with parent 2. F displaces A, A displaces D, D displaces G, and G displaces F. This is a cycle - FADG. These alleles assume the same position in the 2, i.e., C. C in parent 2 displaces B in parent 1 and B displaces C. This is a second cycle - BC. The positions of B and C in the offspring are determined by the second parent. Switching back to parent 1, there is one more cycle - HE. The positions of H and E in the offspring are the same as parent 1.

    Parent 1:   FBCAHGDE

    Parent 2:   ABCDEFGH

    Child: FCBAHGDE

B.3 r-OPT Crossover

Crossover rules can be specifically designed to utilize domain knowledge. r-OPT is designed to incorporate distance information in the traveling salesman problem. Each offspring is generated from $r > 1$ parents with r-OPT crossover. The first allele is chosen arbitrarily, say from the first position of the first parent. For each subsequent allele there are, in general, r choices. For each parent, locate the allele most recently placed in the offspring. Next, find the first following allele, searching circularly, that is not already in the offspring. Consult a distance table to determine which of the chosen alleles has is the closest to the allele most recently placed in the offspring and place it in the offspring. The example that follows is of 2-OPT using the distances in Table B.1.

    Parent 1:   ACGFBDE

    Parent 2:   GEFDCBA

    Child: ACBGFDE

Table B.1. Distances Between Points

	A	B	C	D	E	F	G
A	-	38	12	80	42	20	14
B	38	-	51	32	83	68	10
C	12	51	-	22	91	73	59
D	80	32	22	-	15	29	60
E	42	83	91	15	-	44	75
F	20	68	73	29	44	-	34
G	14	10	59	60	75	34	-

Scene recognition using genetic algorithms with semantic nets

C.A. ANKENBRANDT, B.P. BUCKLES and F.E. PETRY

Center for Intelligent and Knowledge-based Systems, Department of Computer Science, 301 Stanley Thomas Hall, Tulane University, New Orleans, LA 70118, USA

Received 19 June 1989

Abstract: A model for genetic algorithms with semantic nets is derived for which the relationships between concepts is depicted as a semantic net. An organism represents the manner in which objects in a scene are attached to concepts in the net. Predicates between object pairs are continuous valued truth functions in the form of an inverse exponential function ($e^{-\beta|x|}$). $1:n$ relationships are combined via the fuzzy OR (Max[$\cdots$]). Finally, predicates between pairs of concepts are resolved by taking the average of the combined predicate values of the objects attached to the concept at the tail of the arc representing the predicate in the semantic net. The method is illustrated by applying it to the identification of oceanic features in the North Atlantic.

Key words: Genetic algorithms, feature labelling, semantic nets, fitness functions.

1. Background

Genetic algorithms are a problem solving method requiring domain-specific knowledge that is often heuristic. Candidate solutions are represented as organisms. Organisms are grouped into populations known as generations and are combined in pairs to produce subsequent generations. An individual organism's potential as a solution is determined by a fitness function.

Fitness functions map organisms into real numbers and are used to determine which organisms will be used (and how frequently) to produce offspring for the succeeding generation. Fitness functions often require heuristic information because a precise measure of the suitability of a given organism (i.e., solution) is not always attainable. An example is the recognition (i.e., labeling) of segments in a scene. General characteristics of objects in the scene such as curvature, size, length, and relationship to each other may be known only

This work was supported in part by a grant from Naval Ocean Research and Development Activity, Grant #N00014-89-J-6003.

within broad tolerance levels. That is, there is great variability in the relationships among objects in different scenes.

Semantic nets (SNs) are effective representations of binary relationships between concepts (e.g., objects in a scene). SNs denote concepts via nodes in a directed graph. The arcs are labelled by predicates. We introduce here a representation of an organism whose fitness function evaluation is dependent upon an SN context.

Because relationships (i.e., predicates) relating concepts are not precise, their evaluation is in the form of a truth functional with range [0, 1] rather than the traditional {0, 1}. That is, we use fuzzy logic (Yager, 1975; Zadeh, 1988; Zimmerman, 1985) to combine heuristically the information concerning a particular organism. Thus, we derive genetic algorithms with fuzzy fitness functions (GA/F^3).

2. Genetic algorithms

Genetic algorithms (GAs) are search procedures

Figure 1. Oceanic features (North Atlantic). (a) Segmented image. (b) Original infrared image.

modelled after the mechanics of natural selection. They differ from traditional search techniques in several ways. First, GAs have the property of implicit parallelism, where the algorithm is equivalent to a search of the hyperplanes of the search space, without directly testing hyperplane values (Holland, 1975; Goldberg, 1988). Nearly optimal results have been found by examining as few as one point for every 2^{35} points in the search space (Goldberg, 1986). Second, GAs are randomized algorithms, using operations with nondeterministic results. The results for an operation depend on the value of a random number. Third, GAs operate on many solutions simultaneously, gathering information from all current points to direct the search. This factor mitigates the problems of local maxima and noise.

From a mechanistic view, genetic algorithms are a variation of the generate and test method. In pure generate and test, solutions are generated and sent to an evaluator. The evaluator reports whether the solution posed is optimal. In genetic algorithms, this generate and test process is repeated iteratively over a set of solutions. The evaluator returns information to guide the selection of new solutions for following iterations.

GA terminology is taken from genetics. Each candidate solution examined is termed an organism, traditionally represented as a list. The set of organisms maintained is termed a population, and the population at a given time is termed a generation. Each iteration envolves three steps. First, each organism in the current generation is evaluated, producing a numerical fitness function result. The criteria for evaluation is domain specific information about the relative merit of that particular organism. Better organisms are assigned higher fitness function values. Second, some organisms are selected to form one or more organisms for the next generation. Specifically, the number of copies of each organism selected is directly proportional to its fitness function. Third, some of those organisms selected are modified via genetic operators. Each genetic operator takes the chosen organism(s), and produces a new organism(s). The most common genetic operators include crossover and mutation. This iterative procedure terminates when the population converges to a solution.

The crossover operator takes two organisms selected and combines partial solutions of each. When organisms are represented with lists, single point crossover can be viewed as combining the left hand side of one organism chosen with the right hand side of the other, and conversely. This creates two offspring. The crossover point, that point where the crossover takes place, is randomly determined.

The mutation operator uses a minimal change strategy. It takes a selected organism, and changes the value at one randomly determined position. This corresponds to a tight local search. The offspring produced is identical to the parent except at the mutation point.

3. Genetic algorithm problem model for oceanic feature labeling

Scene recognition is an application for which the GA model we propose is suited. For example, Figure 1(a) is a segmented image of the North Atlantic for which Figure 1(b) is the original image. The lines (referred to here as segments, $s_1, s_2, \ldots$) represent boundaries between warm and cold regions of sea water. The problem is to classify the segments as Gulf Stream North Wall (NW), Gulf Stream South Wall (SW), cold eddies (CE), warm eddies (WE), continental shelf (CS), and 'other' (O).

Relationships which can be expressed as fuzzy truth functions are known to exist within or between classifications. Principal among these are (1) the average width of the Gulf Stream is 50 kilometers, (2) the average diameter of an eddy is 100 kilometers, (3) cold eddies are usually south of the Gulf Stream, and (4) warm eddies are usually north of the Gulf Stream. To these one must add the trivial (yet necessary) relationships such as the south wall is at a lower latitude than the north wall and the known geophysical coordinates of continental shelves.

A scene consisting of classifieation categories $(cat_1, cat_2, \ldots, cat_n)$ and relationships expressed as truth functions $(P_{ij}^{(1)}, P_{ij}^{(2)}, \ldots)$ between categories can be modelled as a semantic net (or, more precisely, an association list). A generic one is shown

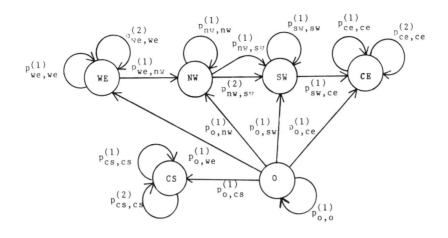

Legend

CS	Contenental Shelf
CE	Cold Eddy
WE	Warm Eddy
NW	North Wall of Gulf Stream
SW	South Wall of Gulf Stream
O	Other

Figure 2. Generic semantic net for oceanic features.

in Figure 2. Segments are attached to the categories via the INST (instance) relation. An allele (or gene) is a category name. An organism is a list of categories, one allele for each segment. For example, given six segments then (NW, NW, SW, CS, CE, O) and (CE, SW, CE, O, O, CS) are representative organisms. Formally, let an asssociation list be defined as $A = \langle V, P \rangle$ where $V = \{\text{cat}_1, \text{cat}_2, \ldots, \text{cat}_m\}$ is a set of categories, and

$$P = \{P_{ij}^{(g)} \mid i, j \leq m, g = 1, 2, \ldots, r_{ij}\}$$

is a set of binary predicates.

These predicates describe the relationships between categories and the ideal relationship between segments assigned to these categories.

Let an organism for spatial labeling be defined as $Q = \langle S, \text{INST} \rangle$, where $S = \{s_1, s_2, \ldots, s_n\}$ is a set of segments, and $\text{INST}: S \to V$ is a function.

Crossover operators

There are three applicable crossover operators. These include single point crossover, two point crossover, and varying multiple point crossover (Booker, 1987). Crossover operators require the imposition of a total order on the segments in S. Let $s_i < s_j$ if $i < j$; $s_i = s_j$ if $i = j$; $s_i > s_j$ if $i > j$. Denote by INST_{Oi} the instance mapping for organism O_i.

Single point crossover. Given $\langle s_1, s_2, \ldots, s_n \rangle$, choose a random integer k, $1 \leq k < n$. For parent organisms O_1 and O_2 create an offspring, O', such that

$$\text{INST}_{O'}(s_i) = \begin{cases} \text{INST}_{O1}(s_i) & \text{if } i \leq k, \\ \text{INST}_{O2}(s_i) & \text{if } i > k. \end{cases}$$

Two point crossover. Let $\langle s_1, s_2, \ldots, s_n \rangle$ be a circular list. Formally, $\text{succ}(s_i) = s_{i+1}$ ($\text{pred}(s_{i+1}) = s_i$) if $i < n$ and $\text{succ}(s_n) = s_1$ ($\text{pred}(s_1) = s_n$). Choose two random integers, k_1 and k_2. For parent organisms O_1 and O_2 create an offspring, O' such that

$$\text{INST}_{O'}(s_i)$$

$$= \begin{cases} \text{INST}_{O1}(s_i) & \text{if } s_i \in \{s_{k1}, \text{succ}(s_{k1}), \\ & \qquad \ldots, \text{pred}(s_{k2})\}, \\ \text{INST}_{O2}(s_i) & \text{otherwise.} \end{cases}$$

Varying multiple point crossover. For parent organisms O_1 and O_2, create an offspring O' such that

$$\text{INST}_{O'}(s_i)$$
$$= \begin{cases} \text{INST}_{O1}(s_i) & \text{with probability } 0.5, \\ \text{INST}_{O2}(s_i) & \text{with probability } 0.5. \end{cases}$$

Mutation operator

Our mutation operator selects one segment randomly and assigns it to a randomly determined category. Choose two random integers k_1, $1 \leqslant k_1 \leqslant n$, and k_2, $1 \leqslant k_2 \leqslant m$. Remove s_{k1} from its current category in organism O and attach it to cat_{k2} (i.e., set $\text{INST}_O(s_{k1}) = \text{cat}_{k2}$).

Fitness function

For the model, the fitness function is the sum of all satisfied predicates in the semantic net. Let E denote the function. Let $P_i^{(g)}$, be defined as above, with m possible categories. Then

$$E = \sum_{j=i}^{m} \sum_{i=1}^{m} \sum_{g=1}^{r_{ij}} P_{ij}^{(g)} \qquad (1)$$

$P_{ij}^{(g)}$ is a predicate for a relationship between categories, i and j. Each predicate $P_{ij}^{(g)}$ has a corresponding derived predicate, $\text{pred}_{ij}^{(g)}(k,l)$, for an analogous relationship between segments s_k and s_l, where s_k is in category i and s_l is in category j. $P_{ij}^{(g)}$ is interpreted based on the normalized truth value of the derived predicate. Specifically,

$$P_{ij}^{(g)} = \begin{cases} \dfrac{\sum_{s_l} \sum_{s_k} \text{pred}_{ij}^{(g)}(k,l)}{|\text{cat}_i| \times |\text{cat}_j|} \\ 0, \quad \text{otherwise} \end{cases} \qquad (2)$$

where $|\text{cat}_i|$ and $|\text{cat}_j|$ are the number of segments classified as category i and category j, respectively. Because all such predicates are not defined between all possible pairs of segments, the normalizing factor (the denominator) is subject to redefinition on a case by case basis. Alternatives to (2) are described following the description of derived predicates below.

An example of a fuzzy predicate $P_{ij}^{(g)}$ from our domain is the relationship 'is near', where category i 'is near' category j. The corresponding derived predicate $\text{pred}_{ij}^{(g)}(k,l)$ describes the relationship between two segments, s_k in category i and s_l in category j. The sum of $\text{pred}_{ij}^{(g)}(k,l)$ for all possible pairs of segments s_k and s_l is normalized by the maximum possible.

Definitions of $\text{pred}_{ij}^{(g)}(k,l)$ are dependent on the underlying semantics of the problem domain. One approach is to define them propositionally as $\{0,1\}$ if a measurable relationship between s_k and s_l is within or beyond some threshold. A second approach preferred here is to define them as fuzzy truth functions on the interval $[0,1]$. Inverse exponential truth functions are commonly used in fuzzy set theory to measure the 'nearness' of two concepts. Alternative nearness measures are in (Zimmerman, 1985). For example, if the description of $P_{ij}^{(g)}$ contains a nominal value (e.g., the SW is approximately 50 kilometers from the NW) then let X_0 represent the nominal value and

$$\text{pred}_{ij}^{(g)}(k,l) = e^{-\beta|X_0 - X|} \qquad (3)$$

where

X is the observed value corresponding to the same measure (distance, curvature, angle of declination) between s_k and s_l,

β is a constant contrast factor in $[0,1]$ which emphasizes the magnitude of the difference between the observed and nominal value when increased.

There are many situations for which the nearness measure is not bounded by an ideal but the closer to s_k the better. In such cases, X_0 can be replaced by zero in formula (3).

'Not near' or 'as distant as possible' may be measured by the fuzzy complement of (3).

$$\text{pred}_{ij}^{(g)}(k,l) = 1 - f(\ ) \qquad (4)$$

where $f(\ )$ is the right side of formula (3).

Some relationships such as 'above' or 'smaller' are not easily modelled as nearness measures. Such relationships can be considered as ordinary propositional truth values.

$$\text{pred}_{ij}^{(g)}(k,l) = \begin{cases} 1 & \text{if } s_k \text{ and } s_l \text{ are so related,} \\ 0 & \text{otherwise.} \end{cases} \qquad (5)$$

If there is a measure X associated with the relationship and $X_k > X_l$ when the condition is met, the derived predicate of formula (5) can be represented by the ceiling function

$$\text{pred}_{ij}^{(g)} = \lceil (X_k - X_l)/(|X_k - X_l| + 1) \rceil. \qquad (6)$$

For $P_{ij}^{(g)}$, each object attached to cat_i requires $|\text{cat}_j|$ evaluations of $\text{pred}_{ij}^{(g)}$. The multiple evaluations are combined to a single value using fuzzy OR

$$\max_{s_l} [\text{pred}_{ij}^{(g)}(k,l)]; \quad \text{for each } s_k \text{ in cat}_i. \qquad (7)$$

This corresponds to finding the best segment, s_l, that matches the relationship for a given segment s_k. By contrast, the combination rule

$$\min_{s_l} [\text{pred}_{ij}^{(g)}(k,l)]; \quad \text{for each } s_k \text{ in cat}_i \qquad (8)$$

corresponds to fuzzy AND. The heuristic implied by the formula (2) is

$$\sum_{s_l} \text{pred}_{ij}^{(g)}(k,l)/|\text{cat}_j|; \quad \text{for each } s_k \text{ in cat}_i \qquad (9)$$

which corresponds to the average truth functional value of s_k with all s_l segments in cat_j.

Let $f_{ij}^{(g)}(k)$ stand for the segment level combina-

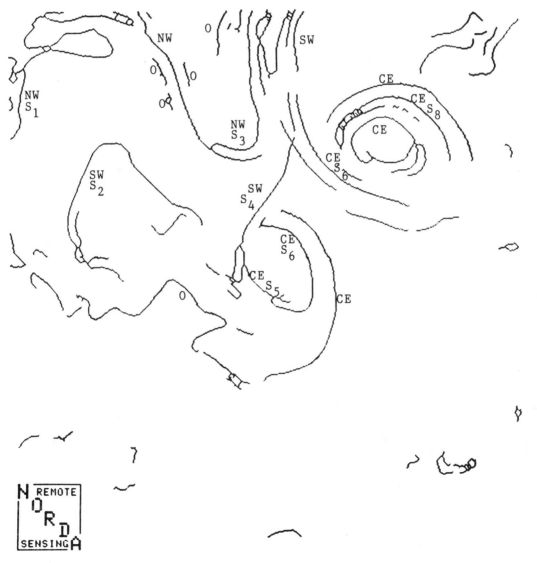

Figure 3. Segmented image with correct labels.

97

tion rule, (7), (8), or (9). Possible aggregation rules to compute $P_{ij}^{(g)}$ are

$$\sum_{s_k} f_{ij}^{(g)}(k)/|\text{cat}_i|, \tag{10}$$

$$\max_{s_k} [f_{ij}^{(g)}(k)], \tag{11}$$

$$\min_{s_k} [f_{ij}^{(g)}(k)] \tag{12}$$

which correspond to average, best, and worst match, respectively. The aggregation rule of formula (10) is the one implied by formula (2).

4. Example

Figure 3 is a reproduction of Figure 1(a) with most segments labelled (correctly). Eight segments are labelled as $s_1, s_2, \ldots, s_8$ and are used below in an example. Table 1 lists and defines all predicates and derived predicates required for the semantic net of Figure 2. The notation $|\text{cat}_h|$ refers to the number of segments that are an instance of category h. The value 0.5 is chosen arbitrarily for β in all derived predicates. The exponential form of derived predicates is used for all relationships except 'north of' where formula (6) is substituted.

Table 1
Predicate descriptions

Predicate	Functional [pred(k, l)]/normalizer	Description
$P_{\text{cs,cs}}^{(1)}$	$\sum_{s_k} \max_{\text{coor}} [\exp(-0.5\,x)]/|\text{cat}_{\text{cs}}|$	near known CS coordinates (distance $= x$)
$P_{\text{cs,cs}}^{(2)}$	$\sum_{s_k} \max_{s_l \text{ where } k \neq l} [\exp(-0.5\,x)]/|\text{cat}_{\text{cs}}|$	near other CS segment (distance $= x$)
$P_{\text{we,we}}^{(1)}$	$(1/|\text{cat}_{\text{we}}|) \sum_{s_k} \max_{s_l} [\exp(-0.5\,|100-x|)]/|\text{cat}_{\text{we}}|$	WE diameter near 100 km (distance $= x$)
$P_{\text{we,we}}^{(2)}$	$\sum_{s_k} \max_{s_l \text{ where } k \neq l} [\exp(-0.5\,x)]/|\text{cat}_{\text{we}}|$	near other WE segment (distance $= x$)
$P_{\text{we,nw}}^{(1)}$	$\sum_{s_k} \max_{s_l} \lceil (X_k - X_l)/(|X_k - X_l| + 1) \rceil/|\text{cat}_{\text{we}}|$	WE north of NW (X_k and X_l are latitudes)
$P_{\text{nw,nw}}^{(1)}$	$\sum_{s_k} \max_{s_l \text{ where } k \neq l} [\exp(-0.5\,x)]/|\text{cat}_{\text{nw}}|$	near other NW segment (distance $= x$)
$P_{\text{nw,sw}}^{(1)}$	$\sum_{s_k} \max_{s_l} [\exp(-0.5\,|50-x|)]/|\text{cat}_{\text{nw}}|$	NW 50 km from SW (distance $= x$)
$P_{\text{nw,sw}}^{(2)}$	$\sum_{s_k} \max_{s_l} \lceil (X_k - X_l)/(|X_k - X_l| + 1) \rceil/|\text{cat}_{\text{nw}}|$	NW north of SW (X_k and X_l are latitudes)
$P_{\text{sw,sw}}^{(1)}$	$\sum_{s_k} \max_{s_l \text{ where } k \neq l} [\exp(-0.5\,x)]/|\text{cat}_{\text{sw}}|$	near other SW segment (distance $= x$)
$P_{\text{sw,ce}}^{(1)}$	$\sum_{s_k} \max_{s_l} \lceil (X_k - X_l)/(|X_k - X_l| + 1) \rceil/|\text{cat}_{\text{sw}}|$	SW north of CE (X_k and X_l are latitudes)
$P_{\text{ce,ce}}^{(1)}$	$\sum_{s_k} \max_{s_l} [\exp(-0.5\,|100-x|)]/|\text{cat}_{\text{ce}}|$	CE diameter near 100 km (distance $= x$)
$P_{\text{ce,ce}}^{(2)}$	$\sum_{s_k} \max_{s_l \text{ where } k \neq l} [\exp(-0.5\,x)]/|\text{cat}_{\text{ce}}|$	near other CE segment (distance $= x$)
$P_{\text{o,o}}^{(1)}$	$\sum_{s_k} \max_{s_l \text{ where } k \neq l} [\exp(-0.5\,x)]/|\text{cat}_{\text{o}}|$	near other O segment (distance $= x$)
$P_{\text{o,}\bullet}^{(\bullet)}$	$\sum_{s_k} \max_{s_l} [1 - \exp(-0.5\,x)]/|\text{cat}_{\text{o}}|$	not near CS, WE, CE, NW, or SW

Table 2
Segment descriptors
(a) Centroid position in fractions of latitude and longitude

Segment	Latitude	Longitude
S_1	39.48	70.04
S_2	38.82	68.69
S_3	39.52	66.84
S_4	38.37	66.67
S_5	37.33	66.72
S_6	37.52	66.06
S_7	38.07	65.81
S_8	39.54	64.86

Table 3
Fitness function values for selected organisms

Organism	Fitness function, E
$O_1 = \langle$NW SW NW SW CE CE CE CE$\rangle$	2.5581
$O_2 = \langle$SW SW NW NW CE CE CE CE$\rangle$	2.0581
$O_3 = \langle$NW SW NW NW CE CE NW SW$\rangle$	2.5001
$O_4 = \langle$SW SW NW CE NW CE CE CE$\rangle$	2.0920
$O_5 = \langle$NW NW CE CE SW NW SW CE$\rangle$	1.0142
$O_6 = \langle$SW CE SW CE SW NW SW NW$\rangle$	1.5830

The default value for any predicate or derived predicate is zero should a denominator evaluate to zero.

The eight segments distinguished in Figure 3 are characterized in Table 2. For this example, we need only the geophysical coordinates, the distances between segment centroids, and the distances between the closest points of segments. A larger, more complete description might also contain the length and degree of curvature of each segment.

Table 3 lists six organisms together with their fitness function values which are computed using the predicates in Table 1. The fitness function is given by formula (2). The combination and aggregation rules are formulas (7) and (12), respectively. Derived predicates are variations of formulas (3) and (4) except 'north of', which is represented by formula (6) with the requisite measure being latitude. Organism O_1 has no segments labelled incorrectly. O_2 has two segments labelled incorrectly. O_3 through O_6 have 3, 3, 5, and 8 incorrectly labelled segments, respectively. The fitness function values correspond roughly to the correctness of the

labelling. Additional predicates (i.e., a more complex semantic net) would improve upon the ordering and separation in most cases.

5. Conclusion

A model for labelling complex scenes via genetic algorithms with fuzzy fitness functions evaluated over semantic nets and GAs is possible. Truth functionals indicating the degree to which specific interfeature relationships are fulfilled are combined at the segment level then aggregated at the category level using fuzzy set operators.

We are currently investigating such issues as the effect of many predicates clustered on one or two categories, alternate forms for the truth functionals themselves, and the crossover rules. Our image set consists of six segmented infrared photographs of the North Atlantic, each photograph having a different degree of observation. Our testbed will consist of a GA algorithm capable of manipulating the alleles' correspondence to the semantic net.

Table 2 (contd.)
(b) Distances between centroids (kilometers, on upper diagonal) and closest proximities (kilometers, on lower diagonal)

	S_1	S_2	S_3	S_4	S_5	S_6	S_7	S_8
S_1	*	127.50	257.55	293.03	342.93	375.45	368.68	416.76
S_2	127.13	*	164.60	168.39	217.12	247.96	243.55	316.35
S_3	–	–	*	115.81	219.21	209.60	167.14	159.20
S_4	–	80.42	31.26	*	104.08	98.13	75.67	186.73
S_5	–	–	–	12.72	*	56.36	104.29	266.84
S_6	–	–	–	15.39	0.00	*	58.67	223.86
S_7	–	–	42.80	16.93	–	–	*	165.51
S_8	–	–	–	35.00	–	–	20.92	*

References

Booker, L. (1987). Improving search in genetic algorithms. In: L. Davis, Ed., *Genetic Algorithms and Simulated Annealing.* Morgan Kaufmann, Los Altos, CA, 61-73.

Goldberg, D.E. (1986). A tale of two problems: broad and efficient optimization using genetic algorithms. *Proc. Summer Computer Simulation Conf.*, July 28-30, 1986, Reno, NV.

Goldberg, D.E. (1988). *Genetic Algorithms in Search, Optimization, and Machine Learning.* Addison-Wesley, Reading, MA.

Holland, J.H. (1975). *Adaption in Natural and Artificial Systems.* Univ. of Michigan Press, Ann Arbor, MI.

Lybanon, M. and R.L. Crout (1987). The NORDA GEOSAT ocean applications program. *John Hopkins APL Technical Digest* 8 (2), 212-218.

Richardson, P.L. (1983). Gulf stream rings. In: A.R. Robinson, Ed., *Eddies and Marine Science.* Springer, New York, 19-45.

Thomason, M.G. and R.E. Blake (1986). Development of an expert system for interpretation of oceanographic images. *NORDA Report 148*, June 1986.

Yager, R.R. (1975). Decision making with fuzzy sets. *Decision Sciences* 6 (3), 590-600.

Zadeh, L.A. (1988). Fuzzy logic. *Computer* 21 (4), 83-93.

Zimmermann, H-J. (1985). *Fuzzy Set Theory and Its Applications.* Kluwer Nijhoff, Dordrecht, The Netherlands.

Genetic Reinforcement Learning with Multilayer Neural Networks

Darrell Whitley, Stephen Dominic and Rajarshi Das
Computer Science Department
Colorado State University
Fort Collins, CO 80523, U.S.A.
whitley@cs.colostate.edu

Abstract

Empirical tests indicate that the genetic algorithms which have produced good performance for neural network weight optimization are really genetic hill-climbers, with a strong reliance on mutation rather than hyperplane sampling. Initial results are presented using genetic hill-climbers for reinforcement learning with multilayer neural networks for the control of a simulated cart-centering and pole-balancing dynamical system. "Genetic reinforcement learning" produces competitive results with AHC, a well-known reinforcement learning paradigm for neural networks that employs temporal difference methods.

1 INTRODUCTION

Attempts to apply genetic algorithms to neural network optimization problems have largely met with modest results. Most of the problems that have been solved are relatively small; though genetic algorithms have been successfully applied to weight optimization for some large problems, recent advances in neural network training algorithms (such as cascade correlation, Fahlman 1990) threaten to overshadow these successes. There are domains, however, where genetic algorithms can make a unique contribution to neural network learning.

We briefly review different strategies for applying genetic algorithms to neural networks and present evidence which suggests that genetic hill-climbers are currently the most effective genetic algorithms for neural net weight optimizations. Furthermore we argue that researchers should seek neural network applications where gradient information is unavailable or hard to obtain. As an example, a genetic hill-climber is used to train a neural network to control an inverted pendulum. We compare the results obtained with the genetic hill-climber to the "adaptive heuristic critc"

(AHC), which uses a temporal difference method to learn to predict failure. The genetic hill-climbing algorithm displays comparable learning times and appears to be robust over a wide range of different learning conditions relative to the nonlinearity of the problem, and the chosen criteria for "failure."

These results are not intended as a general comparison to reinforcement learning using temporal difference methods, or even as a test of "genetic reinforcement learning" versus the "adaptive heuristic critic." Our comparative tests do show, however, that genetic reinforcment learning does offer a viable approach to "neurocontrol" problems.

2 GENETIC HILL-CLIMBERS

In previous work, we have found that genetic algorithms which predominately rely on the recombination of binary encoded strings to drive search can be used to optimize the weights in smaller neural networks, but we have not been able to duplicate this ability on problems with encodings larger than 300 bits (Whitley and Hanson 1989). Our analyses suggest that this "failure" is partially due to the fact that multiple symmetric representations exist for any single neural network. Recombining encodings for functionally dissimilar neural networks can result in inconsistent feedback to the genetic algorithm in the form of high variance associated with hyperplane samples (Whitley, Starkweather and Bogart 1990). Nevertheless, we have been able to "scale-up" a new version of the genetic algorithm to handle relatively large problems. Our results are similar to some of the results reported by Montana and Davis (1989) indicating that larger neural networks can be optimized using genetic algorithms.

Only three major implementation differences exist between the algorithms that have failed to optimize larger nets and those we have used to produced positive results. First, the problem encoding is real-valued instead of binary. This means that each parameter (weight) is represented by a single real value and that recombination can only occur between weights. Second, a much higher level of mutation is used; traditional genetic algorithms are largely driven by recombination, not mutation. Third, a small population is used (e.g. 50 individuals). We have found that a small population reduces the exploration of the multiple (representationally dissimilar) solutions for the same net. The stronger reliance on mutation also helps to avoid this problem since no recombination is involved when mutation occurs. The genetic algorithm we used is a variant of GENITOR (Whitley and Kauth 1988) which uses *one-at-a-time* recombination and *ranking*. These same attributes also characterized the Montana and Davis genetic algorithm. Thus, although the implementation details are not so different from conventional genetic algorithms, the result is a type of stochastic hill-climbing algorithm which we refer to as a "genetic hill-climber."

Using a population of 50, the genetic hill-climber converges to a solution in 90% of 50 runs on a net that adds two two-bit numbers; search times are roughly comparable with, but not superior to back propagation with momentum. The same approach (population of 50, real-value encodings, increased rate of mutation) was used to optimize a large signal detection network. The application is to identify a signal pulse in one of several channels that span a frequency range. This signal detection problem is complicated by 1) a valid signal causes "false signals" to appear in surrounding channels and 2) more than one valid signal may simultaneously exist across multiple channels. Approximately 300 signal samples are present in the training set while several thousand samples exist in the testing set. The genetic algorithm also produced results on this problem competitive with back propagation.

Our analyses indicate that this success does not stem exclusively from the hyperplane sampling processes that are normally viewed as the driving force of a genetic search, but rather involve stochastic hill-climbing. As already noted, the genetic hill-climber has a stronger reliance on mutation and uses a relatively small population. Mutation in the context of one-at-a-time recombination can be thought of as a hill-climbing operator: randomly change some portion of the string encoding the problem; if performance improves, retain the change, otherwise continue mutation. The strong reliance of the genetic hill-climber on mutation and stochastic hill-climbing is demonstrated by incrementally removing the genetic components of the algorithm until it is exclusively driven by stochastic hill-climbing. This is done by shrinking the population size and reducing the use of recombination until only one string is left in the population and mutation is the only operator. Surprisingly, this conversion consistently shows that as the role of the genetic algorithm is reduced the speed of the algorithm increases (the number of evaluations needed to reach convergence is reduced by an order of magnitude on the adder prob-

PopSize	Trials	Convergence
50	42,500	90 %
5	24,000	80 %
1	4,900	72 %

Table 1: *Results for the 2 2-bit adder problem. As population size (PopSize) is reduced faster hill-climbing occurs, but the convergence rate to acceptable solutions (error < 0.0025) decreases. Trials (rounded to the nearest 100) refers to the average trials to convergence only on those cases that did converge.*

lem), but the rate of successful convergence decreases. These results are summarized in Table 1. These results (and other tests) suggest that the global efforts of the genetic algorithm do result in a higher convergence rate, but these same efforts require more evaluations to converge to a solution.

Future researchers should be careful to distinguish between hill-climbing genetic algorithms and hyperplane sampling genetic algorithms since the theoretical foundations of the two are radically different, as are the problems to which they are suited. Goldberg's work (1991) also suggests that there are limitations to the search power of "real-coded coded genetic algorithms" on certain multimodal problems; this should not be a problem, however, when training neural networks.

3 REINFORCEMENT LEARNING

The need for reinforcement learning is based on the fact that for some problems knowledge about what actions are correct or incorrect is not immediate available. Feedback about performance may also be sparse. These kinds of situations preclude the use of relatively simple supervised training algorithms for neural networks such as back propagation. A important application domain of reinforcement learning are control tasks that require unsupervised learning without reliance on any known, a priori, control law. *Back propagation through time* has been applied to such problems, but this is much more complex than simple supervised learning. "Neurocontrol" can be used for the design of automatic controllers that improve their performance by learning from experience.

3.1 The Inverted Pendulum Problem

The inverted pendulum probem is a classic control problem that involves both pole-balancing and cart-centering. This is a well studied control problem which represents an inherently unstable mechanical system of a cart and a pole constrained to move within a vertical plane. At any point in time, the available state information includes the angle of the pole, θ, and the angular velocity of the pole, $\dot{\theta}$, as well as the position of the cart, ρ, and the velocity of the cart, $\dot{\rho}$. The cart is placed on a track of finite length. Using θ, $\dot{\theta}$, ρ and $\dot{\rho}$ as inputs, the output of the neural net is an action to be applied to the cart: either full-push left or full-push right. One of these two actions occurs at each time step.

$$\ddot{\theta}_t = \frac{mg\sin\theta_t - \cos\theta_t[F_t + m_pl\dot{\theta}_t^2\sin\theta_t]}{(4/3)ml - m_pl\cos^2\theta_t} \quad (1)$$

$$\ddot{\rho}_t = \frac{F_t + m_pl[\dot{\theta}_t^2\sin\theta_t - \ddot{\theta}_t\cos\theta_t]}{m} \quad (2)$$

where:
  ρ is the cart position, with a range of $\pm 2.4m$
  $\dot{\rho}$ is the cart velocity, with a range of ± 1.5
  θ is the pole angle
  $\dot{\theta}$ is the angular velocity of the pole
  m_p is the mass of the pole $= 0.1kg$
  m is the total mass of the system $= 1.1kg$
  l is the length of the pole $= 0.5m$
  F is the control force $= \pm 10N$
  g is the acceleration due to gravity $= 9.8m/sec^2$

The system was simulated by numerically approximating the equations of motion using Euler's method with a time step of $\tau = 0.02$ seconds and discrete time equations of the form $\theta(t+1) = \theta(t) + \tau\dot{\theta}(t)$. The sampling rate of the system's state variables was the same as the rate of application of the control force (50 Hz).

There are several interesting aspects of this simulated control task that are relevant for analytical purposes. A failure signal is of course generated when the cart crashes into one end of the track, but a failure signal also is usually associated with a particular angle. For example, in some experiments a failure signal is generated when the pole falls beyond 12 degrees from vertical. The system dynamics can be linearly approximated when θ is less than 12 degrees. For larger angles product expansion terms for θ and $\dot{\theta}$ can not be linearly approximated and the system is nonlinear. The 12 degree limit is commonly used; our experiments attempt to balance the pole over a much larger range of angles, including both linear and nonlinear versions of the problem.

Several researchers have studied this problem. Of particular relevance are those methods which rely on the relatively uninformative failure signal such as Michie and Chambers (1968), Barto and Sutton and Anderson (1983), Selfridge and Sutton and Barto (1985) and Anderson (1989). In the tests reported here, we were particularly interested in training a multilayer neural network for control. Therefore, our simulation experiments, analysis and comparisons have been performed in relation to Anderson's (1989) multilayer adaptation of Sutton's (1984) AHC algorithm.

3.2 Genetic Reinforcement Learning

Supervised training for neural nets implies that for each input in the training set there is a known desired output. But in the case of certain tasks, the correct output may not be known in advance. Consider a sequence of actions on the cart, followed by a failure signal which means the pole has fallen. Let a 1 indicate a push to the right and a 0 a push to the left; "F" indicates failure. Consider the following sequence: 100011110000F. A classic credit assignment problem exists: which of the actions contributed to success and which actions contributed to failure?

The attraction of using genetic algorithms to train neural networks for reinforcement learning is due to the fact that genetic algorithms do not use gradient information. They also compete with algorithms which use only a failure signal to learn. Genetic reinforcement learning can be done using a single net (other approaches use two nets) with performance information as feedback. Furthermore, the genetic based learning algorithm does not have to explicitly evaluate a state in relation to any other state in order to learn. The approach is therefore quite general.

On the pole-balancing problem each real-valued string in the population is decoded to form a network with five input units (four state variables and a constant bias input), five hidden units and one output unit. Five hidden units are used for compatibility with Anderson's (1989) network. The network is fully connected between the input layer and the hidden layer; the input layer is also fully and directly connected to the output unit. All five hidden units also feed into the output unit. Since there are 35 links in the network, each string used by the genetic search includes 35 real values concatenated together.

Before any input is applied to the network, the four state variables are normalized between 0 and 1. Each state variable feeds into one input unit. The action for a particular set of inputs is determined from the activation of the output unit.

A random start state is supplied to the net and an initial action is then applied to the system. The output of the neural net is a value from 0.0 (push left) to 1.0 (push right) using a bang-bang control. The output of the system is a new state which is then reintroduced as a new input to the net. This continues until a failure occurs. In this case, the only monitor or "critic" is an accumulator which determines how long a particular neural network is able to avoid failure; this length of time is a direct measure of fitness. We stopped the genetic search when a net was found that was able to maintain the system without failure for 120,000 time steps (40 minutes of simulated time).

One potential problem with such a simple evaluation criterion is that a favorable or unfavorable start state may bias the fitness ranking of an individual net. We would like to assign a fitness value to a string based on its ability to perform across all possible start states. In reality this is not practical. In our initial experiments we started from one start state and interpreted the output action deterministically; the nets learned, but performance was not robust over a large sample of possible start states. The learning behavior of the net can be improved by interpreting the output "action" probabilistically: in other words, an output of $+0.75$ did not automatically mean that the action should be to push right, but rather that the probability of pushing right is 0.75. This interpretation of the output action allows the net to visit more of the state space and hence learn about more of the problem space. Anderson (1989) also uses a probabilistic interpretation of the output action.

Every algorithm faces the same generalization problem: it must build a decision model for all possible inputs given only a sample of all possible inputs. This problem is not restricted to genetic algorithms, but in genetic algorithms the "generalization problem" is also a noisy evaluation problem. Some set of initial states variables guarantee failure for any sequence of control actions. Networks which receive poor starting states may therefore be ranked lower than networks which receive good starting positions. This creates noise in the ranking function and may result in some nets being lost which are in fact very good competitors. Despite this noise GENITOR performs well in comparison to other learning algorithms. We did try averaging over three trials from different initial starting positions to obtain a better estimate of fitness for strings in the population. This appears to reduce worst case behavior, but does not dramatically change the average learning time. The results reported in this paper therefore are the result of a single learning trial. Methods to deal with this noise in the evaluation function remains a topic of interest; the work of Fitzpatrick and Grefenstette (1988) is particularly relevant.

3.3 Other Genetic Approaches to Control

Genetic Algorithms for learning to control a simulated pole-balancing system have been studied by several researchers. One approach uses predefined partitions of a discrete (binary) state space. When applied to this discretized problem, the genetic algorithm is used to find an appropriate action for each state space partition. The genetic encoding is merely a binary string, where each bit represents an action (push left or right) for each partition of the space. While we are largely interested in reinforcement learning for multilayered neural nets, some aspects of these discrete space approaches are interesting. Odetayo and McGregor (1989) have used this type of approach for pole balancing and cart centering as has Thierens and Vercauteren (1990). The first notable point is that the

entire "vector" of binary values does not have to be correct for the entire space to keep the pole up; the pole need only be started in a favorable position and kept in a favorable position. In Thierens and Vercauteren (1990) experiments only the "critical" bits in the encodings took on correct values; bits for more marginal states were never learned. Another relevant observation is that for problems with a large number of variables it becomes impossible to discretize the space. Consider a problem with 30 variables; even if each variable is binary, the discretized space of 2^{30} partitions is unreasonable.

The multilayer network employed here does not require a discretized state space. This frees the experimenter from having to define the size, shape and placement of partitions in the state space. Furthermore, properly discretizing the state space is part of the task of designing a set of features that are sufficient to learn the control task (Anderson 1986). Our interest is in reinforcement learning algorithms which are capable of learning this feature representation and therefore do not require a discretized state space in order to learn difficult control problems.

4   ADAPTIVE HEURISTIC CRITIC

Anderson's (1989) approach to reinforcement learning uses an adaptive heuristic critic (AHC) composed of an evaluation network, an action network and a learning algorithm. The AHC algorithm attempts to associate "states" and failure predictions using temporal difference methods (Sutton 1988). The action net takes information about the system as input and outputs an action (push left or push right). The evaluation network uses temporal differences methods to learn to predict failure based on the current state of the system. The output of the evaluation net is used to "correct" the output of the action net using a form of back propagation. Temporal differences methods are similar to bucket brigade algorithms; information is passed from one state to the next each time a particular sequence of events occurs (Sutton 1988). Information only gradually reaches those states that are more removed from the failure signal.

The output of the evaluation net is a prediction of failure, with the strength of the output being relative to the expected time to failure. The action and evaluation networks learn simultaneously, resulting in poor initial assignments of credit and blame. As the evaluation net becomes more reliable this information can be used by the "action" net to correct its output behavior in such a way as to avoid failure.

The pole-balance simulator and action network topography were obtained from Charles Anderson. Our best training rates are consistent with the best training rates reported by Anderson (1990).

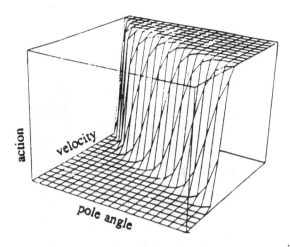

Figure 1: *Plot of pole angle θ, angular velocity θ̇ and the output action on the pole-balancing/cart centering problem using a failure at 12 degrees.*

Seeded Group					
Pop	Best	Worst	Median	Mean	S D
5	1846	17,366	5373	6340	3761
50	16,115	89,615	21,212	24,631	12,699
100	33,979	54,261	40,674	40,815	5031
Restart Group					
Pop	Best	Worst	Median	Mean	S D
5	87	13,104	869	2068	2735
50	225	14,103	3920	4089	2977
100	644	32,057	6223	9380	8457
Normal Group					
Pop	Best	Worst	Median	Mean	S D
5	251	121,988	1614	5971	21,604
50	268	8093	2809	3148	2036
100	332	16,413	3077	3690	2888

Table 2: *Effect of seeding, restarts on learning rate using population sizes (Pop) of 5, 50 and 100. "Normal" implies no restarts or seeding was used.*

5 EXPERIMENTAL RESULTS

Experiments were carried out with failure signals occurring at three different positions of the pole: 12 degrees, 35 degrees and 74 degrees. The 12 degree restriction means that problem has a solution which is is approximately linear. Figure 1 shows the decision boundary learned using the genetic algorithm for the 12 degree problem ploted as a function of the pole angle and the angular velocity. The decision boundaries appear to be very similar to those learned by AHC.

At 35 degrees the problem is nonlinear and contains many start states where it is impossible to balance the pole; empirically we have found it is possible to balance the pole for states up to 39 degrees from vertical, but only if other all other state variables are favorable. At 74 degrees the space is dominated by start states from which it is impossible to balance the pole. The genetic algorithm was able to learn all 3 versions of the problem. And as expected, training time did increase as the problem became more difficult.

5.1 Population Seeding and Restarting

We ran a series of experiments to determine if we could increase the reliability of the genetic hill-climbing algorithm when using small populations. We compared these three strategies using 3 different population sizes of 5, 50, and 100 strings. Each experiment is based on 30 independent runs of the genetic algorithm.

Table 2 shows the effect of population size and various initialization strategies on learning rate using a failure signal at 12 degrees. Best, Median, Worst and Average refer to the number of "starts" before learning (averaged over 30 experiments). "Seeded" populations started with strings that could balance for 100

time steps. This "seeded" strategy involved randomly generating strings until enough strings satisfying the "entry" requirement are obtained. This is analogous to using a initial population large enough to guarantee that X strings satisfy some basic threshold of performance; then the population is reduced to the X best strings. This helped to eliminate the extreme worst case behavior, but uniformly increases the costs of each individual run.

The second strategy (the "restart" strategy) was to pick a random initial population, but if sufficient progress is not displayed early on the population is completely regenerated and the run is restarted. A "restart" occurred if a net had not learned to balance for 600 time steps after 2500 evaluations. This strategy avoids uniform overhead costs, since if a particular run results in fast learning no action is required.

The third strategy shown in Table 2 was to do nothing: run the "normal" genetic algorithm on the initial random population to completion. These tests support the notion that genetic algorithms are fairly robust when left alone. Tests of seeded populations and restarts when using a failure signal at 35 and 74 degrees produced results consistent with those in Table 2; these results are also base on 30 experiments. In subsequent tests we did not use restarts or seeding.

In other tests, an evaluation function based upon the average evaluation resulting from 3 (random) starting positions was used in order to reduce the bias of favorable starting positions. This did not significantly affect the performance of the network. In subsequent experiments we did find that using a harder convergence test had more impact on the consistency of what was learned: continuing training until the system is able to balance the pole 3 times in a row noticeably improves the overall performance of the resulting nets. Both

Learning Rates at 12 degrees					
Method	Best	Worst	Median	Mean	SD
AHC	3866	15,000	4781	6606	3713
Genetic	268	8093	2809	3148	2036

Learning Rates at 35 degrees					
Method	Best	Worst	Median	Mean	SD
AHC	2229	45,000	3192	12,207	16,521
Genetic	602	42,297	4246	6618	7197

Learning Rates at 74 degrees					
Method	Best	Worst	Median	Mean	SD
Genetic	2089	80,268	12,092	17,409	17,378

Table 3: *Comparison of learning rates for AHC and the genetic algorithm (using a population of 50) using 12, 35 and 74 degree failure signals. Results are averaged over 30 experiments.*

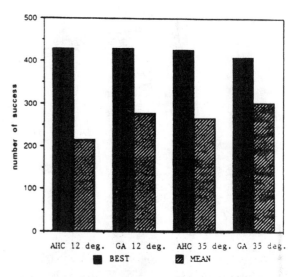

Trained and tested with 12 deg. failure signal					
Method	Best	Worst	Median	Mean	SD
AHC	428	97	179	214	92
Genetic	427	136	267	276	86

Trained and tested with 35 deg. failure signal					
Method	Best	Worst	Median	Mean	SD
AHC	424	65	257	265	96
Genetic	406	122	300	300	75

Figure 2: *Performance of learned function over 625 random start positions for both 12 and 35 degree problems; the genetic algorithm used a population of 50.*

worst case and average case performance is improved by extending the "stopping" criteria from a single success to multiple successes.

While the genetic algorithm did not show the same lack of convergence for the pole balancing problem as it did on the two two-bit adder problem, the results are nevertheless similar. On the pole balancing problem the median training times are lower when using a population of 5, but average and worst case training times are inferior to those achieved with larger populations. In both cases, small population often learn very quickly, but sometimes fail completely (as on the two two-bit adder) or result in very long training times (as on the pole balancing problem).

5.2 Comparative tests

One difference between the genetic algorithm and the AHC algorithm is in their convergence rate. Out of 30 attempts AHC learned a control strategy in only 26 cases (86% convergence) using a failure signal at 12 degrees. The average convergence time (for those cases that did converge) was 5315 trials which is roughly competitive with the average learning time for the various genetic experiments at 12 degrees. The AHC experiments at 12 degrees were run to a maximum training time of 15,000 trials. The average training time for all experiments was 6,606 which is very close to the 6,900 training time reported by Anderson (Anderson 1989) for a single experiment. The genetic algorithm learned 100% of the time and had an average training time of 3,148 trials using a population of 50 strings.

Anderson's original experiments only attempted to learn to balance the pole within the 12 degree range. We also ran experiments using both algorithms with the failure signal extended to 35 and 74 degrees to increase the difficulty of the problem. AHC successfully converged in 24 out of 30 attempts for the 35 degree problem (80%). The experiments were run out to a

maximum of 45,000 trials. These convergence rates are better than those we achieved in initial tests of AHC; working with Charles Anderson we have made some minor changes in the implementation to improve its performance. When the problem was extended to use a failure signal at 74 degrees AHC converged to a successful solution in only 1 out of 30 attempts (learning time, 8261 trials) using upto 100,000 learning trials. There are several parameters (e.g., learning rate, etc.) that must be tuned for AHC and the algorithm is fairly sensitive to these parameters. According to Charles Anderson (personal communication) the algorithm may be overly tuned to the 12 degree problem. Population size is the only parameter we adjusted on the genetic algorithm; our only other parameter–the selective pressure–was set to a linear bias of 1.5 and never tuned.

Table 3 shows the best, average, and worst learning rates for the genetic reinforcement algorithm and AHC when the failure signal is generated at 35 degrees and, for the genetic algorithm, 74 degrees. The genetic algorithm reliably learned in all experiments, even when a failure signal is not generated until the pole reaches 74 degrees. Learning times are slower at 74 degrees, but the increases are reasonably modest.

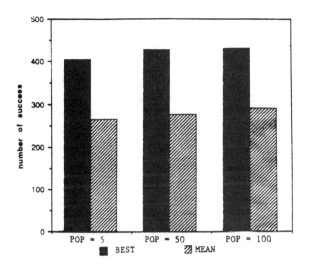

Population size vs. function generalization					
Pop Size	Best	Worst	Median	Mean	S D
5	404	87	260	263	93
50	427	136	267	276	86
100	432	111	297	292	88

Figure 3: *Effect of population size (Pop Size) on performance of the learned function at 12 degrees.*

To further compare the learned function found by the AHC method to the network discovered by genetic search, each system was tested for its ability to balance the pole from 625 random initial state variables. The nets tested were trained on either the 12 or 35 degree version of the pole-balancing problem. Best, average and worse case performance is given for the 30 nets trained by the genetic algorithm; only those nets that learned were tested for AHC. Each net was tested for up to 1000 time steps. Results are given in Figure 2. It is perhaps surprising that the best nets result in failure about 1/3 of the time. This is because many of these initial positions are irrecoverable no matter what control algorithm is used. Figure 3 shows the effect of population size on the ability of the network to balance the pole from 625 random starting positions. The larger population sizes of 50 and 100 tend to both reduce the worst case performance and improve the best case performance. Overall, the larger population sizes produced better results. This observation is consistent with the notion that larger populations should yield better performance when the evaluation (or "fitness") function is noisy (Whitley, Dominic, Das and Anderson 1991).

6   DISCUSSION

There are subtle differences in the information used by the two algorithms, at least in the learning component. In both cases, the "action" net requires input information about the current state in order to produce an output. But one distinction we wish to stress is in the information required for learning. For AHC the evaluation net also requires state information to learn, since without state information there is no prediction of failure. But the genetic algorithm (as opposed to the AHC) does not require state information to update the neural net; it only needs feedback about how long the pole stayed up in order to rank competing sets of weights. This may have important implications for learning to control real-world systems where only time-delayed noisy sensor data is available.

Another difference is that the genetic algorithm only continues to learn as long as failures occur. The reinforcement back propagation that occurs in the action net means that learning continues in the AHC net even when failures are not occurring. Further, the use of temporal difference methods means that the evaluation net is also being updated, even when failures are not occurring. In the genetic approach, updates to the action net occur only after one or more failures. In the genetic algorithm, two networks that avoid failure for an equal number of time steps are equally evaluated. However, the AHC algorithm evaluates networks by the trajectory of states that are experienced. Even though two networks avoid failure for the same number of steps, the evaluations associated with the two nets would differ when the AHC training algorithm is used, favoring the network that drives the cart-pole through more highly-valued states.

Another difference between the genetic algorithm and AHC algorithm is the lack of AHC success when the failure signal occurs at wider pole bounds. This may result from the combination of the incremental learning algorithm used to adjust the weights and the way AHC generalizes. A good prediction of failure is hard to learn when the majority of start states lead to failure. Without a good failure prediction function, a successful control strategy cannot be learned using the reinforcement driven back propagation. The genetic algorithm, because it ranks each network based on performance, is able to basically ignore those cases where the pole cannot be balanced; only the successful cases will obtain the chance to engage in genetic reproduction. For AHC however, these cases provide misleading information which may be learned by the system.

There have been several attempts to apply genetic algorithms to neural network problems. Many of these applications work well for small problems but do not scale up to larger problems. The genetic hill-climbing algorithms described here and used by Montana and Davis work well on large supervised weight optimization problems, but are not as effective as methods such as cascade correlation. We argue that researchers should seek novel applications of genetic algorithms for neural networks such that they are applied in domains where gradient methods are difficult to use. Reinforcement learning for neurocontrol is an application area where it is difficult to directly apply gradient descent methods and where genetic hill-climbing has been shown to produce interesting results. Future work should look at more difficult reinforcement learning problems; genetic reinforcement learning should be also compared to methods such as back propagation through time.

Our purpose in the current study is to demonstrate that genetic hill-climbing algorithms can be used for training neural networks for control problems. The differences between "genetic" reinforcement learning and and other methods for training neural networks using only performance information must be explored more carefully, especially in other application domains. Anderson (1990) discusses several challenging control problems that could provide an initial test bed. We are just finishing the construction of an actual inverted pendulum and will use this to further test the algorithms. We are also interested in ways in which these algorithms might be combined or hybridized. Recently, Ackley and Littman (1991) have combined genetic methods and neural nets for control problems in a different way. They use a genetic algorithm to train the evaluation net, then use the output of the evaluation net to do reinforcement error propagation on the action net. There are also many other ways in which a hybrid system might be developed that uses ideas from both genetic reinforcement learning, AHC and other reinforcement learning paradigms.

Acknowledgements

Our thanks to Charles Anderson for supplying his AHC code and for helpful discussions of the work. This research was supported in part by NSF grant IRI-9010546 and by a grant from the Colorado Institute of Artificial Intelligence (CIAI). CIAI is sponsored in part by the Colorado Advanced Technology Institute (CATI), an agency of the State of Colorado.

References

Ackley, D. and Littman, M. (1990) Interactions Between Learning and Evolution. Submitted to *Proc. 2nd Conf. on Artificial Life.* C.G. Langton, ed. Addison-Wesley.

Anderson, C. W. (1986) Learning and Problem Solving with Multi-layer Connectionist Systems, PhD Dissertation, University of Massachusetts.

Anderson, C. W. (1989) Learning to Control an Inverted Pendulum Using Neural Networks, *IEEE Control Systems Magazine*, vol. 9, no. 3, pp. 31-37.

Anderson, C. W. (1990) A Challenging Set of Control Problems. In: *Neural Networks for Control*, W.T. Miller, R. Sutton and P. Werbos, eds. MIT Press.

Barto, A. G., Sutton, R. S., and Anderson, C. W. (1983) Neuronlike Adaptive Elements That Can Solve Difficult Learning Control Problems. *IEEE Trans. Syst., Man, Cybern.*, SMC-13:834-846.

Fahlman, S. and C. Lebiere (1990) The Cascade Correlation Learning Architecture. *Advances in Neural Information Processing Systems 2.* Morgan Kaufmann.

Fitzpatrick, J.M. and J. Grefenstette (1988) Genetic Algorithm in Noisy Environments. *Machine Learning.* 3:101-120.

Goldberg, D. (1991) Real Coded Genetic Algorithms, Virtual Alphabets and Blocking. *Parallel Problem Solving from Nature* Springer/Verlag, 1991.

Michie, D. and Chambers, R. (1968) BOXES: An Experiment in Adaptive Control. *Machine Learning 2*, E. Dale and D. Michie, Eds., Edinburgh: Oliver and Boyd, pp. 137-152.

Montana, D. and Davis, L. (1989) Training Feedforward Neural Networks Using Genetic Algorithms. *Proc. IJCAI-89*, 1:762-767.

Odetayo, M. and McGregor, D. (1989) Genetic Algorithm for Inducing Control Rules for a Dynamic System. *Proc. Third International Conf. on Genetic Algorithms.* Morgan Kaufmann.

Selfridge, O.G., Sutton, R.S., and Barto, A.G. (1985) Training and Tracking in Robotics, *Proc. IJCAI-85*, pp. 670-672.

Sutton, R. S. (1984) Temporal aspects of credit assignment in reinforcement learning, PhD Dissertation, University of Massachusetts, 1984.

Sutton, R. S. (1988) Learning to Predict by the Methods of Temporal Differences. *Machine Learning* 3:9-44.

Thierens, D and Vercauteren, L. (1990) Incremental Reinforcement Learning with Topology Perserving Maps to Control Dynamic Systems. *Parallel Problem Solving from Nature* Springer/Verlag, 1991.

Whitley, D. and Kauth, J. (1988) GENITOR: A Different Genetic Algorithm. *Proceeding of the 1988 Rocky Mountain Conference on Artificial Intelligence.*

Whitley, D. and Hanson, T. (1989) Optimizing Neural Nets Using Faster, More Accurate Genetic Search. *Proc. Third International Conf. on Genetic Algorithms.* Morgan Kaufmann.

Whitley, D., Starkweather T., and Bogart, C. (1990) Genetic Algorithm and Neural Networks: Optimizing Connections and Connectivity. *Parallel Computing.* 14:347-361.

Whitley, D., Dominic, S., Das, R. and Anderson, C. (1991) Genetic Reinforcement Learning for Neurocontrol Problems. Tech. Report. Dept. Computer Science. Colorado State University.

Annotated bibliography

Interested readers wishing to delve more deeply into topics not fully addressed herein will find the following brief annotated bibliography useful.

1. J.H. Holland, *Adaptation in Natural and Artificial Systems,* University of Michigan Press, Ann Arbor, Mich., 1975.
The original and most widely circulated description of GAs, this text by Holland is considered the most authoritative source with respect to basic theory.

2. D.E. Goldberg, *Genetic Algorithms in Search, Optimization, and Machine Learning,* Addison-Wesley, Reading, Mass., 1989.
This more recent and accessible text benefits from the years of empirical research that followed publication of the Holland monograph.

3. *Genetic Algorithms and Simulated Annealing,* L. Davis, ed., Pitman, London, England, 1987.

4. *Handbook of Genetic Algorithms,* L. Davis, ed., Van Nostrand Reinhold, New York, N.Y., 1991.
These two volumes, edited by Davis, target the practitioner. Davis has collected numerous diverse applications, and dispenses pragmatic information unlikely to be found elsewhere.

About the authors

Bill P. Buckles received his MS in operations research, his MS in computer science, and his PhD in operations research from the University of Alabama, Huntsville. He is a professor of computer science at Tulane University. Previously, he was a faculty member at the University of Texas, Arlington. Prior to that, he was a technical-staff member at Computer Science Corporation, Science Applications Incorporated, and General Research Corporation. At the latter two companies, he performed research in software engineering and distributed processing in conjunction with NASA and Ballistic Missile Defence projects. He has served as principal investigator on various NSF-funded projects as well as other projects supported by state government and industrial research laboratories. He was co-investigator for a NASA/Ames grant in parallel systems analysis, directed by Krishna Kavi, and has published more than 15 journal papers and approximately 35 papers in edited volumes and national conferences. His primary interest is petri-net modeling as it relates to parallel computing. Presently an Editorial Board Member of the *IEEE Transactions on Parallel and Distributed Systems* and an IEEE Computer Society Distinguished Visitor, he is also a senior member of the IEEE and a member of the IEEE Computer Society.

Frederick E. Petry received his BS and MS in physics, and his PhD in computer science, from Ohio State University. He is a professor in the Computer Science Department at Tulane University, where he also serves as co-director of the Center for Intelligent and Knowledge-Based Systems. He has published more than 90 archival and conference papers in various areas of artificial intelligence, computer architecture, and software engineering. His current research interests include knowledge acquisition, the representation of imprecision in databases and expert database systems, genetic algorithms, and specialized hardware division approaches. In addition to serving as technical editor for all IEEE Computer Society videotape projects and member of the IEEE Computer Society Press Editorial Board, he is editor of a new series entitled *Advances in Databases and Artificial Intelligence,* and has served as guest editor for a special issue of *Fuzzy Sets and Systems* on fuzzy information systems and databases. A member of the IEEE, ACM, AAAI, Sigma Xi, Upsilon Pi Epsilon, and Sigma Pi Sigma, he is also listed in *Who's Who in Technology.*

Other Technology Series
from IEEE Computer Society Press

ARTIFICIAL NEURAL NETWORKS

Artificial Neural Networks — Concept Learning
edited by Joachim Diederich
Catalog # 2015. ISBN # 0-8186-2015-3. 160 pages. $30.00 / $24.00 Members

Artificial Neural Networks — Electronic Implementation
edited by Nelson Morgan
Catalog # 2029. ISBN # 0-8186-2029-3. 144 pages. $32.00 / $24.00 Members

Artificial Neural Networks — Theoretical Concepts
edited by V. Vemuri
Catalog # 855. ISBN # 0-8186-0855-2. 160 pages. $20.00 / $15.00 Members

COMMUNICATIONS

Multicast Communication in Distributed Systems
edited by Mustaque Ahamad
Catalog # 1970. ISBN # 0-8186-1970-8. 128 pages. $28.00 / $21.00 Members

MATHEMATICS

Computer Algorithms: Key Search Strategies
edited by Jun-ichi Aoe
Catalog # 2123. ISBN # 0-8186-2123-0. 154 pages. $30.00 / $24.00 Members

Multiple-Valued Logic in VLSI Design
edited by Jon T. Butler
Catalog # 2127. ISBN # 0-8186-2127-3. 120 pages. $35.00 / $28.00 Members

ROBOTICS

Multirobot Systems
edited by Rajiv Mehrotra and Murali R. Varanasi
Catalog # 1977. ISBN # 0-8186-1977-5. 144 pages. $28.00 / $21.00 Members

SOFTWARE

Computer-Aided Software Engineering (CASE)
edited by Elliot J. Chikofsky
Catalog # 1917. ISBN # 0-8186-1917-1. 136 pages. $20.00 / $15.00 Members

Software Reliability Models:
Theoretical Developments, Evaluation, and Applications
edited by Yashwant K. Malaiya and Pradip K. Srimani
Catalog # 2110. ISBN # 0-8186-2110-9. 136 pages. $30.00 / $24.00 Members

Also by Fred Petry

Object-Oriented Databases
edited by Ez Nahouraii and Fred Petry
Catalog # 1929 . ISBN # 0-8186-8929-3. 256 pages. $50.00 / $35.00 Members

For more information or to order call:
1—800—CS—BOOKS

IEEE Computer Society Press Titles

Domain Analysis and Software Systems Modeling
Edited by Ruben-Prieto Diaz and Guillermo Arango
(ISBN 0-8186-8996-X); 312 pages

Formal Verification of Hardware Design
Edited by Michael Yoeli
(ISBN 0-8186-9017-8); 340 pages

Groupware:
Software for Computer-Supported Cooperative Work
Edited by David Marca and Geoffrey Bock
(ISBN 0-8186-2637-2); 500 pages

Hard Real-Time Systems
Edited by J. A. Stankovic and K. Ramamritham
(ISBN 0-8186-0819-6); 624 pages

Knowledge-Based Systems:
Fundamentals and Tools
Edited by Oscar N. Garcia and Yi-Tzuu Chien
(ISBN 0-8186-1924-4); 512 pages

Local Network Technology (Third Edition)
Edited by William Stallings
(ISBN 0-8186-0825-0); 512 pages

Microprogramming and Firmware Engineering
Edited by V. M. Milutinovic
(ISBN 0-8186-0839-0); 416 pages

Nearest Neighbor Pattern Classification Techniques
Edited by Belur V. Dasarathy
(ISBN 0-8186-8930-7); 464 pages

New Paradigms for Software Development
Edited by William Agresti
(ISBN 0-8186-0707-6); 304 pages

Object-Oriented Computing,
Volume 1: Concepts
Edited by Gerald E. Petersen
(ISBN 0-8186-0821-8); 214 pages

Object-Oriented Computing,
Volume 2: Implementations
Edited by Gerald E. Petersen
(ISBN 0-8186-0822-6); 324 pages

Parallel Architectures for Database Systems
Edited by A. R. Hurson, L. L. Miller, and S. H. Pakzad
(ISBN 0-8186-8838-6); 478 pages

Reduced Instruction Set Computers (RISC)
(Second Edition)
Edited by William Stallings
(ISBN 0-8186-8943-9); 448 pages

Software Engineering Project Management
Edited by Richard H. Thayer
(ISBN 0-8186-0751-3); 512 pages

Software Maintenance and Computers
Edited by David H. Longstreet
(ISBN 0-8186-8898-X); 304 pages

Software Design Techniques (Fourth Edition)
Edited by Peter Freeman and Anthony I. Wasserman
(ISBN 0-8186-0514-6); 730 pages

Software Reuse — Emerging Technology
Edited by Will Tracz
(ISBN 0-8186-0846-3); 400 pages

Software Risk Management
Edited by Barry W. Boehm
(ISBN 0-8186-8906-4); 508 pages

Standards, Guidelines and Examples on System
and Software Requirements Engineering
Edited by Merlin Dorfman and Richard H. Thayer
(ISBN 0-8186-8922-6); 626 pages

System and Software Requirements Engineering
Edited by Richard H. Thayer and Merlin Dorfman
(ISBN 0-8186-8921-8); 740 pages

Test Access Port and Boundary-Scan Architecture
Edited by Colin M. Maunder and Rodham E. Tulloss
(ISBN 0-8186-9070-4); 400 pages

Visual Programming Environments:
Paradigms and Systems
Edited by Ephraim Glinert
(ISBN 0-8186-8973-0); 680 pages

Visual Programming Environments:
Applications and Issues
Edited by Ephraim Glinert
(ISBN 0-8186-8974-9); 704 pages

Visualization in Scientific Computing
Edited by G. M. Nielson, B. Shriver, and L. Rosenblum
(ISBN 0-8186-8979-X); 304 pages

Volume Visualization
Edited by Arie Kaufman
(ISBN 0-8186-9020-8); 494 pages

REPRINT COLLECTIONS

Distributed Computing Systems:
Concepts and Structures
Edited by A. L. Ananda and B. Srinivasan
(ISBN 0-8186-8975-0); 416 pages

Expert Systems:
A Software Methodology for Modern Applications
Edited by Peter G. Raeth
(ISBN 0-8186-8904-8); 476 pages

Milestones in Software Evolution
Edited by Paul W. Oman and Ted G. Lewis
(ISBN 0-8186-9033-X); 332 pages

Validating and Verifying Knowledge-Based Systems
Edited by Uma G. Gupta
(ISBN 0-8186-8995-1); 400 pages

For further information call toll-free 1-800-CS-BOOKS or write:

IEEE Computer Society Press, 10662 Los Vaqueros Circle, PO Box 3014,
Los Alamitos, California 90720-1264, USA

IEEE Computer Society, 13, avenue de l'Aquilon,
B-1200 Brussels, BELGIUM

IEEE Computer Society, Ooshima Building, 2-19-1 Minami-Aoyama,
Minato-ku, Tokyo 107, JAPAN

IEEE Computer Society
VIDEO COLLECTION

Available from IEEE Computer Society Press